Solving Writing Problems with Easy Mini-Lessons

Written by
Dolores Hudson

Editor:
Alaska Hults

Illustrator:
Kate Flanagan

Project Director:
Carolea Williams

Table of Contents

Introduction 3

Writing Lesson Format 4

Assessment Ideas 6

Mini-Lessons

Problem: *Students do not maintain a writing environment*
Solution: *Rehearsing Procedures* 9

Problem: *Students fail to use punctuation or correct spelling errors*
Solution: *Understanding Conventions* 15

Problem: *Students don't know what to write about*
Solution: *Generating Ideas* 27

Problem: *Students do not write a clear beginning, middle, or end*
Solution: *Developing Organization* 38

Problem: *Students wander from their topic*
Solution: *Maintaining Focus* 57

Problem: *Students write simple, uninformative sentences*
Solution: *Improving Description* 67

Problem: *Students overuse common words*
Solution: *Enhancing Word Choice* 83

Introduction

Do your students have trouble thinking of a topic to write about? How many run-on sentences have you read this week? Are you ready to retire students' overused words, such as *fun, very,* and *nice?* Whether you are looking for a fun way to exchange writing ideas, a surefire way to encourage your students to build description into their writing, or a new way to teach your students to work productively, your answers are here.

Solving Writing Problems with Easy Mini-Lessons offers a wide range of mini-lessons that target six different skill areas that are common problem areas for developing writers. Designed to fit into your existing writing program, this resource provides many new ideas and a few "tried and true" activities with a new spin or flavor.

Each section starts with basic lessons and ends with lessons for the more fluent writer. Reproducibles are included for some lessons to provide writing samples, introduce novel formats, or make your preparation easier. Several lessons include additional tips—entitled *Break It Down*—to assist you in meeting the needs of students who require more background, further practice, or additional assistance from an adult.

Literature links are provided at the end of most mini-lesson sections. Because learning to write is linked to learning to read, and because young writers enjoy mimicking the styles of the authors they love to read, each suggested title includes a summary of the book and an activity that offers students the opportunity to apply the skill through the integration of literature.

Although students are reading chapter books, illustrated storybooks are often referenced because they most closely match the kind of writing your students produce. Some sections also include titles of phonics-based readers in a storybook context so every student in your class has a book he or she can read independently to practice these skills. There are whole-class activities as well as activities for individuals or small groups.

The ideas from *Solving Writing Problems with Easy Mini-Lessons* fit into any writing lesson format that includes writing, editing, revising, and conferencing sections. This book invites students to choose their own topics for practicing skills, but many of the lessons can be easily adapted to topics you assign as well.

Writing Lesson Format

Time

Schedule your lessons at approximately the same time every day. Begin with shorter, highly structured periods at the start of the year and gradually lengthen the amount of time students are given to write and conference.

Materials

Provide the following materials:

- a place to put works-in-progress, such as a decorated file folder
- plain white and three-hole-punched lined paper
- pencils, highlighters, and colored pens
- publishing materials such as crayons, colored pencils, scissors, and construction paper
- a computer center, if one is available

The mini-lessons in this book fit into a three-part writing period: the mini-lesson, individual writing and conferencing, and sharing.

Structure

Mini-Lesson

Mini-lessons direct the attention of your young writers to a specific aspect of writing. They are pulled from the student's needs, writing continuums, and teacher judgment. Most effective mini-lessons are

- short.
- focused on one topic.
- responsive (topic is determined by the needs of the students).
- repeated (several times throughout the school year as needed).

The mini-lesson ideas in this book are not intended to be taught in sequential order. Assess your students throughout the writing period, and choose the mini-lesson that best addresses your students' needs.

Individual Writing and Conferencing

During this time, students may start new drafts, add to or revise existing drafts, or publish completed works. As students are writing, it is helpful for them to receive some feedback about what they are writing. One of the easiest ways to do this is through conferencing, which gives you the opportunity to work one-to-one with each student in the class. Conferences are more effective when limited to a discussion of one skill. Here are some areas you may focus on during your discussion:

- Conventions: Has the writer made clear his or her meaning using correct spelling and punctuation?
- Organization: Is the order of events clear?
- Beginning: Does the lead catch the attention of the reader?
- Middle: Are sequence words used to communicate the order of events?
- Ending: Does the piece have an ending that leaves the reader satisfied?
- Focus: Is the student clear about his or her topic?
- Description: Where could more details be added to clarify or enrich the story?
- Word Choice: Has the student replaced any overused words (e.g., *fun, good, then*)?

To ensure that every student's needs are met (a challenge in a class of more than 30), invite parent volunteers to conference with students. Choose parents who are available on a regular basis, and assist them by giving them a list of skills to focus on (such as the one above). Though parent volunteers are helpful, be sure students conference with you at least once in a while.

Sharing

Approximately four to six students share with the class their finished pieces or works-in-progress. Compose a schedule or invite students to sign up for sharing dates.

Tip: Write numbers on small index cards and place them in order on your desk. Have all students who have completed a first draft take a number.

Assessment Ideas

Keeper Journal and Reflection

One way to track students' progress is to invite them to write once a month in a Keeper Journal. Staple 10–12 sheets of paper between two pieces of construction paper to make a journal for each child. The first time you have students write in their journal, tell them their journal will be a record of the progress they are making in learning to write. Explain to students that this journal will be part of what you use to show their growth in writing to their parents. At the end of the writing period, collect the journals. When you encounter a piece of writing that is difficult to read because of poor spelling, punctuation, or grammar, invite the author to read it to you. Write the "translation" on sticky notes so you don't change the student's writing. Spend a few minutes with each student, and make compliments about what you see him or her doing well. Be a writing cheerleader! Then set new goals for growth with the student. Use the Keeper Journal for making anecdotal notes for conferencing with parents and for showing the student how far he or she has grown.

How Did It Go Today?

Tell students that all writers have successful days as well as days of poor progress. Then ask them to rate how they did that day as a writer on a scale of one to three. For example, a three means they were focused and worked hard. A two means they struggled, but worked through it. A one means they had a hard time writing today. Invite students to share their experiences that day. For example, a student who spent the whole writing period brainstorming a topic instead of writing may inspire a discussion on how to budget time during the writing period. Finally, encourage students to think silently for a few minutes and set goals for the next day's work.

Developing a Rubric

One of the most effective ways to help students improve in writing is to develop with them specific criteria for what makes a *good* piece of writing. Then discuss an *OK* piece of writing. Finally, discuss the attributes of writing that *needs improvement.* (Instead of using the terms *good, OK,* and *needs improvement,* consider using the same codes as your report card.) Encourage students to use this information to guide them in producing good writing.

Message Books

Message Books are a fun way to briefly assess young writers' use of conventions. They differ from journals in which the student writes an entire piece on a topic of his or her choice. With Message Books, students write a short, conversational reply to your question, instead of a longer, developed piece of writing on a topic of their choice. Here are some guidelines for using Message Books:

- Write the same question in each Message Book, choosing a new question each month.
- Choose a consistent time for the class to work on the books.
- Set standards for appropriate response length.
- Distribute a Message Book to each student.
- Invite students to read and respond to your question, and have them use appropriate conventions in their writing.

Assess each student's response for correct usage of conventions and encourage students to make necessary changes to clarify their meaning. Support students who need to make more than one change.

The Editing Checklist

An editing checklist reproducible is provided on page 8. Initially, invite each student to complete the checklist while conferencing with you. When your class has gained fluency with the checklist, invite each student to use the checklist to guide his or her editing before conferencing with you. Alternatively, invite students to brainstorm a list of the skills and conventions they expect to use in their writing, and use this list to create a checklist that is tailored to the class's needs. This list can be updated as the class gains new skills and confidence.

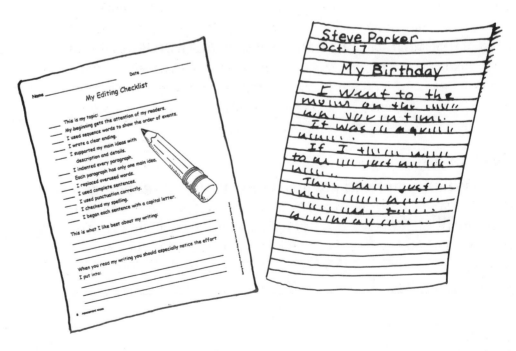

Name _____   Date _____

My Editing Checklist

_____ This is my topic: _____

_____ My beginning gets the attention of my readers.

_____ I used sequence words to show the order of events.

_____ I wrote a clear ending.

_____ I supported my main ideas with
       description and details.

_____ I indented every paragraph.

_____ Each paragraph has only one main idea.

_____ I replaced overused words.

_____ I used complete sentences.

_____ I used punctuation correctly.

_____ I checked my spelling.

_____ I began each sentence with a capital letter.

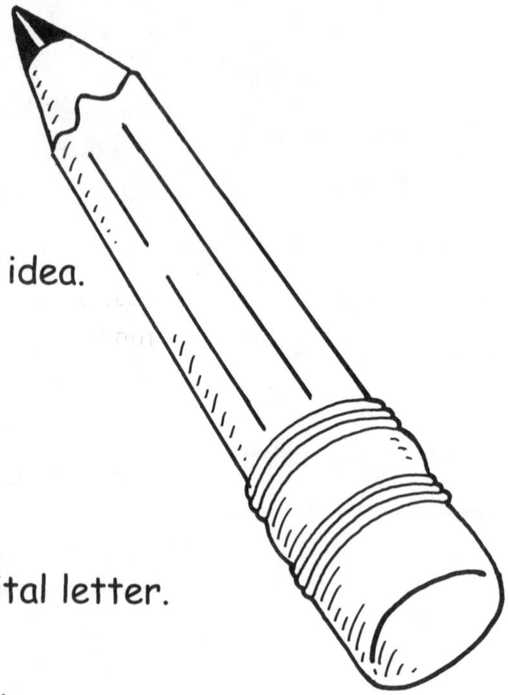

This is what I like best about my writing:

_____

_____

_____

When you read my writing you should especially notice the effort
I put into:

_____

_____

_____

Solving Writing Problems with Easy Mini-Lessons © 1999 Creative Teaching Press

Rehearsing Procedures

> Practice, practice, practice.
> —your mother

When you'd like to have students read their writing to each other, but you're concerned they won't know how to keep the focus on the writing, try one of the lessons on sharing. Instead of having students who spend the writing period sharpening pencils, obtaining an eraser, or finding paper, teach one of the lessons on expectations. The writing programs in which students flourish have clear expectations and consistent consequences. Just as good writing is practiced, so is a good writing program. These mini-lessons are designed to teach the expectations of your writing program and give students the opportunity to practice meeting them.

Establishing Expectations

Demonstrate how and where materials such as pencils, pens, paper, scissors, or glue are to be obtained, used, and returned. Model proper conduct for tasks that require students to leave their desks or interact with other students. Have volunteers demonstrate this conduct, and have the class critique their efforts. Finally, have the students practice a mock writing period. Assess their understanding of your expectations, and praise them for a terrific run-through.

Consider the following tips:

- Supply a decorated can with sharpened pencils to avoid pencil sharpening during quiet time.
- Use editing pens in colors that stand out.
- Have a checkout system so you know where the materials are.
- Provide students with a simple filing system in an accessible place for storing works-in-progress and completed papers.

Teaching Smooth Transitions

Evaluate when your students will need to transition from one place to another. For example, your students may start on the floor together for a mini-lesson, then go to their desks to write quietly, and finally return to the floor to hear each other's writing. Introduce the signal you will use to aid transition. Model how students should respond to the signal. Then question your students to be sure they understand your expectations. Invite volunteers to demonstrate a smooth transition, and then have students practice together as a class.

Try one of these signals:
- bell
- lights (flick them on and off)
- clapping rhythm
- small finger cymbals
- music (sung or recorded)
- attention spot (This is a spot on the floor where you stand only when you want students' attention. Hold your hand up and silently count to five, by which time they should be seated and attentive.)

Lend an Ear

Have a volunteer who wants to share wait out of the hearing of the rest of the class. Tell the remainder of the class that, while the student shares, they will demonstrate both appropriate and inappropriate listening behavior. Discuss how these behaviors look and sound. Explain that they are to demonstrate appropriate listening behaviors when the student begins sharing until you give a subtle signal such as picking up a book or playing with a paper clip. At this signal, students should begin to fidget, whisper to a neighbor, play with something in their desk, or demonstrate other inappropriate behaviors (within reason). Invite the volunteer back into the group, and have him or her proceed with sharing. Have students listen and then not listen at your signal. When the student has finished his or her sharing, redirect the class to good listening, and ask the volunteer to tell about what he or she experienced. Ask the student who shared if he or she noticed the moment the students stopped listening. Invite students to consider which sort of an audience they would prefer for their own sharing. Offer a new volunteer the chance to share, while the class practices their good listening skills. Ask this student to tell how it felt to have the class listen attentively to his or her sharing.

Author! Author!

Write on chart paper the following steps for sharing:

1. The author reads the story of his or her choice to the rest of the class.
2. The author then asks the audience *What do you like about my story?*
3. The author calls on three classmates.
4. After listening to the responses, he or she says *Thank you.*
5. The author asks *What can I do to my story to make it even better?*
6. The author calls on three additional classmates.
7. After listening to the responses, he or she says *Thank you.*

Read aloud the steps with the class, and then model the process once with a piece of your own writing. Discuss your demonstration with the class, and then invite volunteers to model the process with their own work. Coach the volunteers and the class as they practice until you are sure they understand the process.

Try one of these suggestions:

- Have a place for the students to present their writing.
- Invite students to use a microphone (if one is available).

Have a bag or box of student names from which the reader pulls names of respondents.

Respectful Responses

Part One

Post a blank piece of chart or butcher paper, and invite students to brainstorm listeners' responsibilities when an author is sharing. Record their responses. Encourage students to consider the listeners' goal as improving the author's writing while being considerate of his or her feelings. When you are satisfied the class has generated a complete list of listeners' responsibilities, discuss any rules you would like to emphasize.

Part Two

Photocopy on an overhead transparency the Respectful Responses reproducible (page 13). Invite students to recall the listeners' goal discussed during Part One. Have students read the reproducible with you. Where appropriate, discuss new vocabulary such as *express, opinion,* and *consider.* Tell students that each section contains a list of ways the listener can start to tell his or her ideas or ask questions about the author's writing. Invite students to think of other times these respectful responses can help them express their opinions. For example, students might suggest solving a problem on the playground, doing group work, solving a disagreement with a friend, or talking to their parents.

Part Three

Set a time limit, and have a volunteer share briefly. Encourage three students to use the reproducible to respond appropriately to the writer's sharing, and offer coaching wherever needed. Repeat until you are confident that the class has the understanding of how to choose a respectful response. Invite students to work in small groups, listen to classmates share their writing, and respond using the respectful responses. When time is up, invite students to drop a note in a small box on your desk whenever they use these respectful responses outside of sharing. Devise a quick way to acknowledge these students, such as reading the notes at the end of the day and complimenting the students.

Respectful Responses

Expressing an Opinion

I believe . . .

You might think about . . .

I think . . .

It seems to me that . . .

Maybe you could . . .

Here's what I think you should do . . .

Asking for More Information

I have a question about that.

Would you read that again?

Would you say more about that?

Do you have an example of that?

Disagreeing

I don't agree with you because . . .

You might feel differently, but . . .

You might consider it this way . . .

Solving Writing Problems with Easy Mini-Lessons © 1999 Creative Teaching Press

What Good Thinking Sounds Like

After you have brainstormed details related to a topic, display a blank overhead transparency and model the thought process of writing. As you compose a complete paragraph, refer to your brainstormed details, and think aloud about each step that you make. When you have completed the paragraph, invite students to tell you what they observed. Record their observations on chart paper under the heading *What Good Thinking Sounds Like*. Display the chart for future reference.

What Good Thinking Sounds Like
1. Thinking about writing, nothing else
2. Has a certain way of writing, checks off each step
3. Rereads what is written, checks for mistakes while writing

Time Left on the Clock

Invite students to brainstorm a list of things to do if their writing is complete before the writing period ends. Give each student a sticky note on which to write at least one idea from the list. Invite students to place their sticky note in their writing folder as a tactile reminder the next time they complete their writing early. Then post your class list for future reference.

Possibilities include the following:

- Look around the room for an idea to add to your writing.
- Read what you have written and pretend that you are sharing. What else would the class want to know about?
- Read your writing from another day.
- Close your eyes and think about what else you could add.
- Read a book quietly.
- Begin publishing the final draft.
- Sign up for a conference.

Understanding Conventions

Often the search proves more profitable than the goal.
—E. L. Konigsburg

When you see run-on sentences, or what might appear to be a disregard for standard spelling, pull out one of these mini-lessons. Conventions are the visual cues of writing, and their purpose is to clarify the author's meaning. These lessons motivate students to make the extra effort by emphasizing the power of conventions to make their writing attractive to the reader. Follow these lessons with individual or small-group conferences.

Why Use Conventions

Photocopy on an overhead transparency the My Cat, Carl reproducible (page 16), and display it on an overhead projector. Tell students *Conventions are actions done in a certain, accepted way. There are conventions at the dinner table, called manners, such as sitting properly in your chair, and conventions when we meet people, such as shaking hands or saying* Pleased to meet you. *There are also conventions in our writing that help the reader understand the writer. One convention in English is that our words start on the left side of the page and go to the right side.* Invite students to contribute additional conventions. Use the My Cat, Carl reproducible as visual clarification when needed.

Some of the conventions in the reproducible include

- paragraph indentation
- commas in a series
- spacing
- punctuation with quotes
- margins
- capital letters for proper nouns
- punctuation showing possession

Record students' suggestions on chart paper to post for future reference. Tell students that when they use these conventions consistently they clarify the meaning for their readers. Invite students to choose a convention they currently use inconsistently (such as correct spelling or proper end punctuation) and decide to improve their use of it.

 Conference with a student, and focus on the conventions the student is using successfully. Then have the student choose one convention to add to that piece of writing, and acknowledge the child for the clarity that convention adds to the piece.

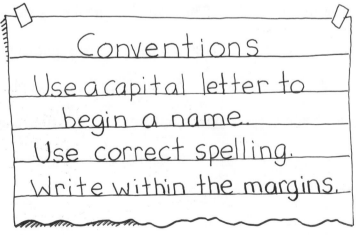

Conventions
Use a capital letter to begin a name.
Use correct spelling.
Write within the margins.

My Cat, Carl

It has been a year since I received my cat, Carl. It was my birthday. I saw him at the grocery store. He was in a box with his brothers and sisters. A boy and his mother were giving them away. Carl was mewing. He looked straight at me and waved his paw as if he were saying, "Pick me!" So I begged my dad right there to let me have him.

"Let's ask your mom first," he sighed, because cats make my mom sneeze.

Luckily, we had mice behind the dryer at this time. Mom kept trying to catch them, but they were clever mice and stayed free. Mom thought having a cat, even one that made her sneeze, might get rid of the mice. I promised to encourage Carl to chase mice and keep him out of Mom's bedroom.

Dad, Mom, my little brother, and I went back to the grocery store and picked up Carl. By then, there was only one other kitten.

"Please, Mom?" begged my brother. Carl's brother was so cute Mom said, "Yes." Then we all went inside the store and bought kitty litter, litter boxes, cat food, and some flea powder.

I don't think Carl and his brother, Pete, caught the mice. I think the mice just moved out because our house was suddenly not such a great place to live. Now it is a year later and Carl and Pete are big, fat, happy cats.

Solving Writing Problems with Easy Mini-Lessons © 1999 Creative Teaching Press

Capital Letters

As you conference you have the opportunity to teach individual students a particular rule of capitalization. In the context of their own writing, students often are quick to find value in the rule and apply it easily and more consistently than if they had learned the rule as part of a group lesson. This lesson builds on that quick mastery by further inviting the student to take on the role of class expert for a lesson and to share his or her knowledge with the class. For example, a student who has just learned to capitalize the first letter of the name of a place can demonstrate this rule to the class. Help students keep the lessons brief by following this format:

1. Photocopy the student's finished piece on an overhead transparency.
2. Have the student tell the class the rule for capital letters that he or she will demonstrate.
3. Have the student circle the capital letters with a colored overhead marker to show the class all the places in the writing where he or she applied this rule.
4. As the student circles each letter, have him or her tell how that example fits the capitalization rule being demonstrated.

Why Spelling Counts

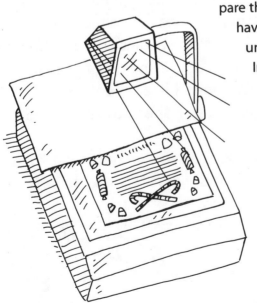

Photocopy on an overhead transparency the Making Choices reproducible (page 18). Tell students you are going to show them two stories and you want to know which one they would like to read first. Display each story, covering the other, for about 15 seconds. Then cover both stories. Ask students which story they would prefer to read and why. Invite students to consider whether their choices are based on the story's elements or the writer's use of conventions. Invite volunteers to compare the first few sentences of each version. Continue having students compare the remaining sentences until students realize that these are the same story. Invite students to consider the effect of correct spelling and the ease with which they could decode and enjoy the correctly spelled story. Encourage students to review as a group ways they improve the spelling in their own work, such as checking a word wall, sounding words out, asking a partner, or using a dictionary. Invite students to return to their own writing and edit for spelling. Have them use every method and resource available to them to correct their spelling.

Making Choices

My Gingrbred Hows

Hi! My nam is Marie. Iam go to tell you abuot my gingrbred hows. I was mad ot ov gram krakers, frsting, an alot ov candy.

The gram krakers wer for the wolls an ruf. At first, I had trubl poting the frusting on. The gramm krakers kep braking! Latr, I had the frist part ov my gingrbrid hows don. What wus lef to do wus the dekerating an the ruf.

So far, my gingrbred hows lukd like a rektangle wishing it wer a hows. Then it wus time to put the ruf on. It wasent to hard.

Finuly, it wus time to decorat. I usd candi ribon for a boarder. I put to candi kans up and mad the tips tuch. I was fun.

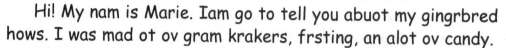
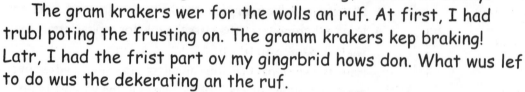
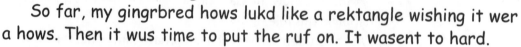

My Gingerbread House

Hi! My name is Marie. I'm going to tell you about my ginger-bread house. It was made out of graham crackers, frosting, and a lot of candy.

The graham crackers were for the walls and roof. At first, I had trouble putting the frosting on. The graham crackers kept breaking! Later, I had the first part of my gingerbread house done. What was left to do was the decorating and the roof.

So far, my gingerbread house looked like a rectangle wishing it were a house. Then it was time to put the roof on. It wasn't too hard.

Finally, it was time to decorate. I used candy ribbon for a border. I put two candy canes up and made the tips touch. It was fun.

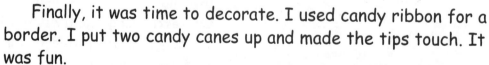

Solving Writing Problems with Easy Mini-Lessons © 1999 Creative Teaching Press

 **Break It Down** Tape-record students as they sound out a word, and then let them hear themselves say the word back slowly. Coach students to identify the individual phonemes they hear. Model writing the letters that represent those sounds, and then have the students practice this.

Sounding Out a Word

Tell students about a time when you wanted to write a word but you weren't sure how to spell it. Invite students to raise their hand if they have been in this situation. Ask students to recommend strategies they used to solve this problem. When a student mentions sounding out the word, tell the children that you have found this helpful, too. Invite volunteers to think of a word and model sounding out the word. Praise students who slow down their speech to emphasize each segment of the word to hear the individual sounds that make up the word. Next, encourage students to try some of the following ways to sound out words:

- Say the word like a ghost—stretch the word out using a scary voice.
- Stretch the word out like a rubber band.
- Say the word like a sheep—stretch the word out using a wooly stutter.

Sound out several words together. Start with easy, three-letter words, and then use longer words suggested by students. Invite students to use words they recently read or tried to write.

Delving through the Dictionary

Photocopy the Delving through the Dictionary reproducible (page 21).
Display for students the interior of a dictionary, and tell them that the book
is used to find meanings of words and to check the spelling of words. Invite
students to contribute words for you to locate. Read the guide words at the
top of the dictionary pages aloud, and model using them to locate the
correct page. Read the spelling of the word and the primary definition. Then
ask students to suggest words in the context of a specific sentence so you
can model how to choose the correct spelling (e.g., *plane* vs. *plain*) if there is
more than one meaning of the word. Invite volunteers to take your place and
accept new words in context to find in the dictionary. Then, invite students to
work in pairs to practice using the dictionary by having them complete the
Delving through the Dictionary reproducible. Review it together. Encourage
students to use the dictionary to check words they are unsure how to spell.
After students have learned to use a thesaurus, you may want to repeat this
lesson with fluent writers and model how to find the meaning of new words
they discover in the thesaurus.

Break It Down Work with a
small group of
students. Give each
student a dictionary. Give students a common blend (e.g., *br,
dr, st,* or *tr*), and have them
use the guide words to find
the words that begin with
that blend. Invite students to
dictate to you three words
that begin with that blend,
and ask students to use the
guide words to locate the
three words they dictated.
Have each student show the
group the location of the word
and tell how he or she used the
guide words to find the word.

Delving through the Dictionary

Name _____   Date _____

Part 1: Locate these words in the dictionary and write the guide words located at the top of the page.

family _____ _____   flag _____ _____

jump _____ _____   corner _____ _____

Part 2: Locate the italicized words in the dictionary and read the definitions. Then decide if the word has been spelled correctly, as it is used here. If the word is spelled correctly, write the definition on the line. If the word is spelled incorrectly, write the correct spelling and its definition on the line.

1. We are going to the beach in an *our*. __hour__ __60 minutes_____

2. She likes to eat *carats*. _____

3. My *aunt* is coming to visit. _____

4. We pitched our *tense* in the woods. _____

Part 3: Locate each word, write the page number you found it on, and check its spelling. If the spelling is wrong, write the correct spelling on the line under *Correct Spelling*. If the spelling is correct, write the page number and leave the line in the *Correct Spelling* column blank.

	Page Number	Correct Spelling
1. peple	_____	_____
2. iritate	_____	_____
3. complane	_____	_____
4. connect	_____	_____
5. sqeeze	_____	_____

Frantic Phrases

Organize students in small groups, and give each group a clipboard and paper or a small white board or chalkboard. Tell students they will be writing complete sentences. On an overhead transparency, write and display a phrase. Invite each group to copy the phrase on their paper or board and turn it into a complete sentence. Stop often to discuss the students' answers, and praise groups as you hear them discussing what they are adding and why. Each time you present this lesson, you can choose to highlight a specific part of the sentence, such as the subject, predicate, nouns, verbs, adjectives, adverbs, direct objects, or other parts of sentence construction you may have covered in a previous lesson. Give groups points for each sentence they complete correctly, and tell students that punctuation counts. When a group offers a phrase that is still an incomplete sentence, invite the class to contribute the element of the sentence that is missing.

Try some of the following phrases:
- to eat on Sunday
- why not
- fell into the canyon
- almost silently Nancy
- weighed 32 pounds
- ate up the disgusting green pudding

When the lesson is over, applaud the groups for their efforts and encourage students to read their writing and look for incomplete sentences to finish.

Periods

Photocopy on an overhead transparency the Stop That! reproducible (page 23). Invite students to imagine that a period is like a stop sign because it tells the reader when the writer has come to the end of a complete thought. Invite the class to read the first three lines of the reproducible together and discuss where the periods should be placed. Use a red marker (representing a stop sign) to place periods in the appropriate places. Encourage students to tell how they know where each period belongs. Remind students to capitalize the first letter of the next word. Continue in this manner through the rest of the reproducible. When the class has completed the entire story, invite students to return to their own writing and put periods in the places they want the reader to stop.

Stop That!

Once upon a time there was a mouse named Chester Chester had a passion for cheese one day he came upon a cheese shop in his travels and decided to go inspect it Chester entered the shop very cautiously "i hope there are no cats here," he thought, twitching his nose suddenly a huge hand swooped down and grabbed Chester "oh, no!" he squeaked Chester saw the face of a kind old woman

"oh little mousie!" she smiled "you must be hungry have some cheese"

Chester rubbed his paws happily "this must be heaven," he thought

Swiss
4.99/lb.

Getting Rid of *And*s

Copy on the chalkboard a pair of sentences linked by *and* to form a run-on sentence. Invite the class to discuss whether or not the *and* can be replaced by a period. Have students listen to whether the sentence sounds complete without the *and*. Use the extra examples listed below for review on another day.

Examples where *and* cannot be replaced by a period:

- Isaiah, Jesse, and Max swam at the beach and had a great time.
- In the fall I play soccer and football.
- I learned to ride my bike when I was four years and to rollerskate when I was five.
- My dad rides motorcycles on the street and in the dirt.

Examples where *and* can be replaced by a period:

- The three boys swam all morning at the beach and they all said that they had a terrific time.
- In the fall I am the goalie on my soccer team and I am also the quarterback for my football team.
- I learned to ride my bike when I was four years old and I learned to rollerskate when I was five.
- My dad rides motorcycles on the street and in the dirt and my mom just rides her motorcycle on the street.

And Then What?

Display and read aloud an overhead transparency of the And Then What? reproducible (page 25). Reread the first two lines but this time do not say the *and*s. Pause to show where the period should be placed. Invite a volunteer to circle all of the *and*s in the story while the class keeps count. Encourage volunteers to cross out each *and,* insert a period, and capitalize the first letter of the next sentence. Invite students to think of *and* like a flashing yellow light, which warns that a period may be needed. Challenge students to see if they can get rid of an *and* in one of their stories. It is important to note that sometimes *and* needs to be used in sentences. The rule of thumb is that if the sentence doesn't sound right without the word *and,* leave it in.

And Then What?

I did a lot of work in the garden with my mother this weekend and it was very hard and we planted seeds and we pulled out weeds like dandelions and we used our hoes to till the soil so we could push bulbs deeper into the dirt and we went to the store to buy a new hose and we brought it home and Mom hooked it up and soaked the entire garden and it was exciting to think of all the plants that we will be growing!

Dialogue

Photocopy on an overhead transparency text from a book with dialogue. Display the transparency, and ask students *What conventions tell you that people are talking?* Make a list of the conventions used with dialogue, including

- Spoken words have quotation marks around them.
- Ending punctuation is included before the last quotation mark.
- Question marks and exclamation points are used instead of a comma where appropriate.
- A new paragraph begins every time a new character starts talking.
- The writer often names the character who is talking.

Display a comic strip in which two characters are talking. Have the class convert the comic strip into a short story with written dialogue. Record student suggestions on an overhead transparency. When the class has completed their story, invite students to work in pairs to write a brief dialogue for the two characters. For further practice, invite students to bring in comic strips from home to convert into a short story with dialogue.

Possessives

The day before this lesson, invite students to bring in a favorite object for show and tell. Write *This is* on a sentence strip and display it. Tell students that we show the reader that an object belongs to someone or something by adding an apostrophe to a noun that ends in *s* and *'s* to a noun that does not. Invite a volunteer to come to the front of the class, display his or her show-and-tell item, and briefly tell about it. Repeat the rule for showing possession, and write a phrase on a sentence strip to show how it applies to this student (e.g., *Alphonso's baseball glove*). Display the sentence strip next to the *This is*

sentence strip, and ask the class to read aloud the completed sentence (e.g., *This is Alphonso's baseball glove*). Invite the volunteer to place his or her object and sentence strip together on a table. You will soon have a visual review of two ways that possession can be shown. For example, *Jesse's glass, Hannah's watch, Jesus' game, Iris' bear.* If you don't have enough students with names that end in *s*, do a few imaginary examples as you go, or invite "guest stars" such as Mrs. Williams, the principal, or Mr. Jenkins, the kindergarten teacher, to share an item with the class.

Generating Ideas

Write what you like;
there is no other rule.
—O. Henry

One of the most common complaints students share with their teachers is that of not being able to come up with a topic. The following mini-lessons help students develop strategies for brainstorming ideas. Teaching students how to generate their own ideas makes them active participants in the creative process and provides them with a feeling of pride for and ownership of their work.

Imaginary Backpack

Ask students how they think writers get ideas for stories. Show students examples of books that come from an author's life. Tell students that many writers get story ideas from their own lives. Share some examples of story ideas that come from your own life, write these ideas on separate sentence strips, and put them into a backpack as you talk a little about each one. Then have the students imagine they each hold a backpack full of their own experiences. Encourage volunteers to describe one or two experiences in their imaginary backpack. Ask students to carefully tighten the straps and check the fit. Distribute a copy of the Imaginary Backpack reproducible (page 28) to each student. Have students read through the questions on the backpack and work in pairs or small groups to add five ideas to their Imaginary Backpack's list of experiences. When students are done, have them store their paper in their writing folder for future use. Encourage students to keep their imaginary backpack on at all times to collect writing ideas. Invite students to pull ideas from their imaginary backpack when they have writing to do. Consider presenting the class with a real backpack students can take home one at a time and return with an item to show and tell about. Encourage students to write about the objects they bring in the backpack.

The following are books that came from the author's own experience:
  Circle of Gold by Candy Dawson Boyd
  Fourth Grade Rats by Jerry Spinelli
  I Love You the Purplest by Barbara M. Joosse
  Nim and the War Effort by Milly Lee
  Owl Moon by Jane Yolen
  Roxaboxen by Alice McLerran
  The Whales' Song by Dyan Sheldon

Imaginary Backpack

Name _____   Date _____

What's in Your Imaginary Backpack?

What is special about you?
What are your hobbies?
What can you tell about the people in your family?
What makes you happy? sad? excited?

Solving Writing Problems with Easy Mini-Lessons © 1999 Creative Teaching Press

Jot Lists

At the start of the year, invite students to share writing ideas. Record these ideas on chart or butcher paper, and offer students the opportunity to list ideas that are appealing to them. This list is the start of each student's Jot List—a place to jot down ideas. Next, provide students with time to add to their list. Remind students to list each idea in just a few words. Have them put their list in a place where they may easily refer back to it when they need a topic. Invite students to pick one of their ideas to use as a writing topic.

Break It Down Invite students who have difficulty integrating auditory information to tape-record their conversation so they can refer back to the tape for details.

Buddy Up

Give students five minutes to think silently of a topic idea. Then invite students to choose a buddy, or assign them to pairs. Have students decide in each pair who is Buddy A and who is Buddy B. Have Buddy A describe a writing idea and Buddy B respond with recommendations for improving the writing idea. Ask students to switch roles. Finally, have students write a piece that incorporates some or all of their buddy's ideas. Alternatively, have each buddy share his or her own story idea (no critique is offered) and then write out the piece he or she just described.

Snap Shot

Display a real or paper camera, and share a photograph of an event at school or from home. On chart paper or an overhead projector, model writing about the experience in the photograph. Refer to the photograph to help students notice details. Have each student bring a picture from home to write about. Give each student a copy of the Snap Shot reproducible (page 30) for displaying his or her photo and finished written piece. Alternatively, build a file of photographs from memorable events to help students recall experiences they want to write about.

Snap Shot

place photo here

Solving Writing Problems with Easy Mini-Lessons © 1999 Creative Teaching Press

Brainstorming Topics

Demonstrate how to brainstorm writing topics by thinking aloud. Write topics on an overhead projector as you mention them. For example, you might describe some less substantial topics and point out why they are not usable. Then demonstrate how to come up with a usable idea based on a common item in the classroom. After you are finished talking, invite students to comment on the kinds of decisions you made and how you made them. Discuss questions students may have, and then encourage them to brainstorm new topics with the techniques you modeled.

Falling Stars

Have each student write three writing topic ideas on a half sheet of paper. At your signal, have students crumple their paper into a ball and toss it lightly into the air. Invite students to scramble to get a new ball, carefully open it, and record on a new sheet of paper the topic ideas they find. Repeat this process twice more, each time having students throw the ball they gathered, until they have a list of new ideas. Have students use one of the new ideas to begin writing.

Walk 'n' Talk

Photocopy and distribute to each student a copy of the Walk 'n' Talk reproducible (page 32). Have students think of a few writing ideas and write those at the top of the paper. Invite students to circulate around the room until you give a signal (e.g., bell, music, lights on/off). While students circulate, have them share with each other the ideas they have already written in the topic box and write the new ideas they gather in the bottom portion of the sheet. When time is up, ask students to return to their seat and add this paper to their writing folder. Encourage students to use an idea from this sheet in their daily writing.

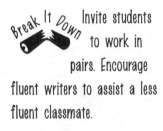

Break It Down Invite students to work in pairs. Encourage fluent writers to assist a less fluent classmate.

Walk 'n' Talk

Name _____ Date _____

Directions: Write your topic ideas in the box.

1. _____   6. _____

2. _____   7. _____

3. _____   8. _____

4. _____   9. _____

5. _____   10. _____

Directions: Ask classmates for topic ideas.
Record those ideas here.

1. _____   7. _____

2. _____   8. _____

3. _____   9. _____

4. _____   10. _____

5. _____   11. _____

6. _____   12. _____

Solving Writing Problems with Easy Mini-Lessons © 1999 Creative Teaching Press

Writing from Experience

Ask a student volunteer to describe an experience he or she has not yet had, such as graduating from high school or going to college. Then, drawing on your knowledge of the student, ask about activities he or she does often. For example, invite the student to describe his or her baseball practice, time at recess, or favorite pastime. Repeat this activity with other volunteers. Encourage students to tell as much as they want. Ask students which topics were easiest to talk about—those which the students had already experienced or those which they had not. Ask students which topics would be easier to write about. Have students write about a recent experience.

Surfing for Ideas

Model how looking around the room can help a writer think of new topics. For example, say *When I look at _____, it makes me think of a time when _____ happened to me.* Ask volunteers to demonstrate this process by having them use various visual cues in the classroom to generate topic ideas. For example, a student might say *Scissors remind me of a time when I cut my own hair and my mother was mad* or *The aquarium reminds me of my pet.* Finally, have the class take out their Jot Lists (page 29) and add two new ideas based on what they see in the classroom. Encourage students to choose one of those ideas to write about today.

Pick a Prop

Choose a prop such as a stuffed animal, a loose key, or a child's plastic cup. Hold up your prop, and ask students to look carefully at it. Ask students to suggest writing ideas inspired by the prop. For example, hold up a telephone, and ask if anyone is reminded of an event or story idea. Share from your own experience, and invite students to share as well. Invite students to bring in objects they want to tell the class about. Encourage students to write about their object and then read the completed writing and display the item as a prop.

Unsticking Stuck Students

Tell students that writers often share tricks to help other writers. Ask students to tell how they come up with new ideas. Write their advice on chart or butcher paper. Strategies students generate may include the following:

- Think about what you did over the weekend.
- Reread some of your old stories.
- Think of something that you did in school.
- Use the Frame the Topic reproducible (page 61) to find a topic in an old piece of writing.
- Look at your Jot List (page 29).

Encourage students to use one of these methods to come up with a new topic to write about today. Post the class-created chart where students may refer to it.

Topics from A–Z

List the alphabet in capital letters down the left margin of a large piece of butcher paper, and display it. Invite students to suggest a topic for each letter. If the class gets stuck on the last few letters, invite students to look for topics in encyclopedias or a dictionary until the list is complete. Then encourage students to choose a topic on which to write. Post the finished pieces around the A–Z list. Alternatively, give smaller groups a portion of the alphabet to brainstorm topics, and have each group contribute their ideas to one master alphabet list. Mix up the letters to give each group equal work.

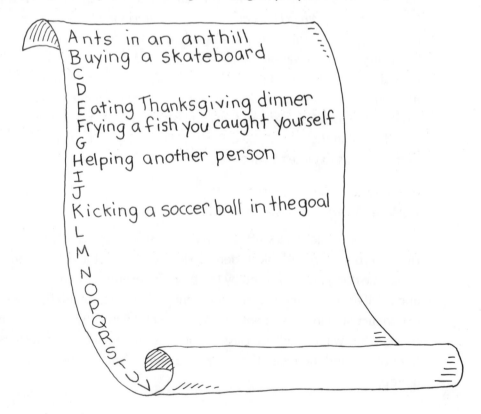

Using Literature to Generate Ideas

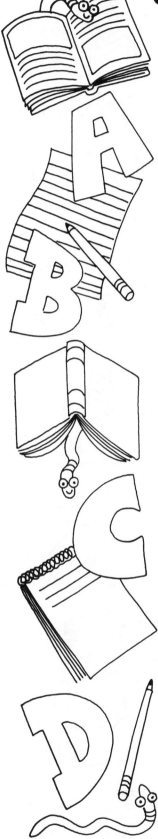

Alexander and the Terrible, Horrible, No Good, Very Bad Day by Judith Viorst
This book is about a boy who cannot escape his bad day. Invite students to share when they have had a bad or a perfect day. Suggest that they write about it or add it to their Jot List.

Amazing Grace by Mary Hoffman
In this story, Grace gets encouragement from her grandmother and is chosen to play Peter Pan in the school play. Have a discussion about a time when students were encouraged by a caring person to try a new activity. Use this discussion as a springboard for student stories.

Bus Riders by Sharon Phillips Denslow
This story tells about events on a bus ride to school. Invite students to write about their own bus ride or other exciting transportation experiences.

Can't You Sleep, Little Bear? by Martin Waddell
This story is about an adorable bear who has a hard time falling asleep. Encourage students to talk about when they can't fall asleep. Invite students to write about a night when they had trouble getting to sleep.

Click, Click by Margaret Allen (Creative Teaching Press)
This book features cute panda characters taking pictures at the park. Invite a small group of students to tell what they would take pictures of if they had a roll of twelve-exposure film. Encourage each student to choose one of these twelve topics for his or her writing. This book also focuses on the *qu* and *ck* phonemes.

Footprints and Shadows by Anne Wescott Dodd
This book has a repeating, intriguing phrase that focuses on footprints and shadows that change over time. Invite students to use the phrase in their own writing.

The Gardener by Sarah Stewart
This story is told through the letters of a girl writing home. She stays the summer with her grumpy uncle, Jim, but comes prepared with a suitcase full of items for growing flowers. Invite students to write about times when they cheered someone up or ways they can cheer people up.

Ira Sleeps Over by Bernard Waber
This story is about how a friend provides some extra security for someone spending the night away from home for the first time. Invite students to write about their favorite stuffed animal, blanket, or toy.

Let's Be Friends Again! by Hans Wilhelm
In this book, a little sister sets her big brother's turtle free. After being angry, the brother decides that being friends with his sister is more fun. Have a discussion about similar experiences students may have had. Encourage students to write about a time when they had a special time with a relative or friend.

Life Is Fun by Nancy Carlson
This story lists simple instructions for having a happy life. Invite students to write their own book of simple instructions for how to be a friend, what to do when disappointed, how to show kindness, or how to control anger.

Night Tree by Eve Bunting
This story is about a family who visits the forest every year at Christmas to decorate the same tree with treats for forest animals. Invite students to write about a favorite family tradition.

Nim and the War Effort by Milly Lee
Nim gathers newspapers for a contest at her school but loses them all to a bully. In solving her problem of how to still win the contest she must find a balance between the values of her loving Chinese grandfather and those of her San Francisco neighborhood. Invite students to write about a time they stood up to a bully or had to explain their actions to an adult.

Owl Moon by Jane Yolen
In this beautiful story, a young child goes owling in the woods at night with his father. Invite students to tell about a favorite evening with a parent. Tell students that the use of specific details helps draw the reader into the story.

The Rag Coat by Lauren Mills
This is a story about a determined Appalachian girl who gets a coat made of rags. Each rag represents a moment in the lives of the people around her. Invite each student to write an autobiographical story on a square of colored construction paper and decorate it. Display the squares together as a quilt of stories.

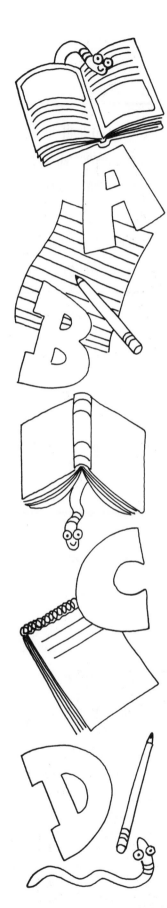

The Rainy Day Band by Margaret Allen (Creative Teaching Press)
This book is about a family of bears who put together a delightful band using common household objects for instruments. Invite students to imagine an instrument they make themselves. Encourage students to write about their instrument and the music that they would make. This book also focuses on contractions.

Roxaboxen by Alice McLerran
In this book, the children build a magical world where rows of stones become roads and boxes become furniture. Invite students to tell the class about a time when they used their imagination to have fun.

Sally's Room by M. K. Brown
A little girl's bedroom comes to life and asks to be cleaned. Have students discuss why their bedroom is special to them. Invite students to write about their bedroom.

Something from Nothing by Phoebe Gilman
This is a story about the relationship between a boy and his grandfather. Invite students to write about their relationships.

The Storm Book by Charlotte Zolotow
In this book, a summer storm invites people to stop and listen to it. Read aloud this book, and relate it to a recent stormy day. Help students personalize the topic by asking them questions about their experiences on that day.

Truck Tricks by Margaret Allen (Creative Teaching Press)
This story shows trucks in a great race with a surprising finish. Encourage students to describe their ideal truck or other form of transportation such as a car, a bike, or skates. Then have students write about that form of transportation and add an illustration to the finished product. This book also focuses on blends such as *tr, gr, dr, cr, fl*, and *sp*.

When I Was Little: A Four-Year-Old's Memoir of Her Youth by Jamie Lee Curtis
The four-year-old in this book revels in all she can do now that she is no longer a baby. Invite students to tell the class about their new skills, and encourage them to reflect on their successes. List students' responses on a chart, and then suggest that students follow the author's pattern to write about their growth.

Wilfred Gorden McDonald Partridge by Mem Fox
In this book, a young boy befriends an elderly woman in a nursing home who is rumored to have lost her memory. Encourage students to write about a memory, or invite students to make their own memory boxes and then write about each item in the box. Take students to a nursing home, and encourage them to present their memory box. Invite the residents to write back to your class with their own memories.

Developing Organization

Somewhere between *Once upon a time* and *The End* students' writing can take many detours. Authors organize their writing so the reader will know where to find the main idea, key details, and concluding thoughts. Young writers recognize well-organized writing when they read it, but only learn to organize their own writing through direct instruction. The mini-lessons in this section incorporate a variety of skills from basic paragraph and essay brainstorming to the use of a hook to gain the reader's interest and a smooth conclusion to provide the reader with a satisfying ending.

> There's no limit to how complicated things can get, on account of one thing always leading to another.
> —E. B. White

A Story Is like a Plane Ride

Invite volunteers to tell the class about their experiences on a plane. Then tell students that they are going on an imaginary plane ride. Have them pantomime buckling in, and tell them *A plane ride is like a well-written story. A plane ride starts with a smooth takeoff during which we are eager to go on our flight. A good story starts with an interesting beginning that makes the reader want to continue. Once the plane is in the air, we get to watch movies and have a snack* (pantomime eating peanuts from a bag). *Most of the trip is spent in the air. This is just like the details in a piece of writing. Most of the events and information are told in the details of the story. Here comes our careful landing! The plane ride ends with a safe landing. A story should also have a smooth conclusion so the reader knows the story is over without having to say* The End. Invite students to recall the stages of a plane ride and how the stages are like the parts of a written piece. Then encourage students to examine their works-in-progress for a clear topic, details, and a smooth conclusion. A picture of a plane with key words written on it can be a visual reminder of the analogy.

Events, Information, Description

Interesting Beginning

Smooth Conclusion

The Hamburger Paragraph

Tasty Ideas

Name _____ Date _____

Start with a topic sentence
that covers all you want to say.
Spaghetti

Give the reader three juicy details.

One Cheesy Two Messy

Three Lots of meatballs

I love it!
End with a filling conclusion.

40 minutes...

Break It Down With a small group, model making a list on lined paper of sentences from the key words students wrote on the reproducible. Then have the students arrange those sentences in a paragraph on a new sheet. Encourage students to add this step between brainstorming and writing in paragraph form until they gain enough fluency to write in paragraph form directly from the reproducible.

Tell students there are three parts to a paragraph:

- The topic sentence tells the reader what the paragraph is about.
- Detail sentences reveal descriptive information about the topic.
- The concluding sentence wraps up the paragraph.

Display a transparency of the Tasty Ideas reproducible (page 40), and tell students they can remember to include each part by picturing a hamburger. The buns represent the topic and concluding sentences, and the fillings represent detail sentences. Invite the class to suggest a topic, and fill in each section of the transparency with key words. Then demonstrate how to write a complete paragraph using the student responses. Have students compose topic and detail sentences from key words and agree upon a strong concluding sentence. For their daily writing activity, divide the class into small groups, and give each group a photocopy of the Tasty Ideas reproducible. Invite each group to choose a topic, brainstorm key words for their group's reproducible, and work together to write a complete paragraph. Have groups present the work they did together on the Tasty Ideas reproducible first and then read aloud their finished paragraph.

Tasty Ideas

Name _____   Date _____

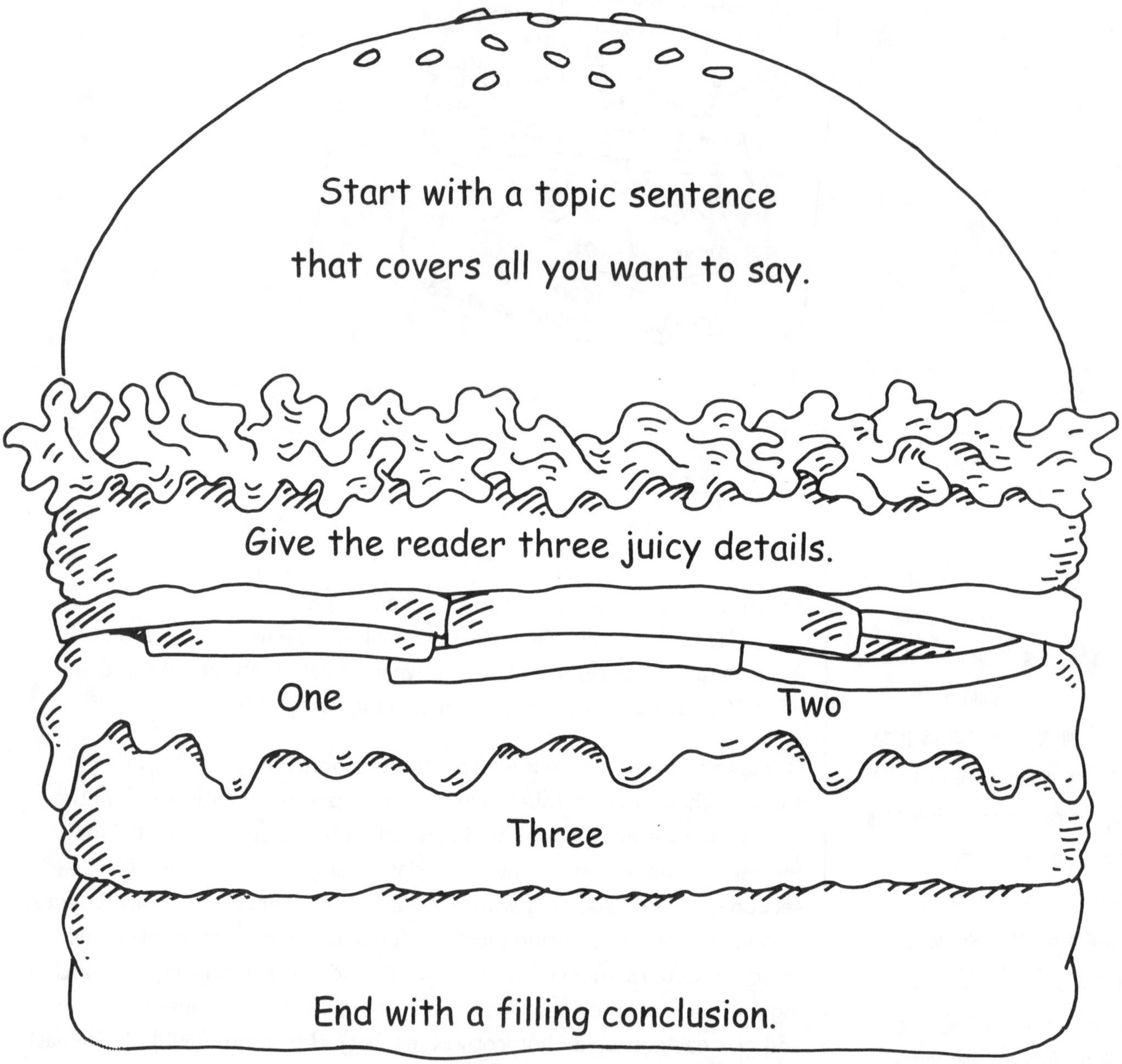

Start with a topic sentence
that covers all you want to say.

Give the reader three juicy details.

One   Two

Three

End with a filling conclusion.

Solving Writing Problems with Easy Mini-Lessons © 1999 Creative Teaching Press

A Hand Full of Details

Part 1

The Hand, Star, Me, and Sun reproducibles on pages 42–45 are variations on the classic word web used to organize the thoughts of young writers. Photocopy the reproducible of your choice on an overhead transparency, and photocopy on plain white paper a class set of the reproducibles for students. Display the transparency, and model how to complete the reproducible by writing a topic in the center. Encourage students to suggest details that pertain to the topic. Write these details next to the word *Detail* on the transparency.

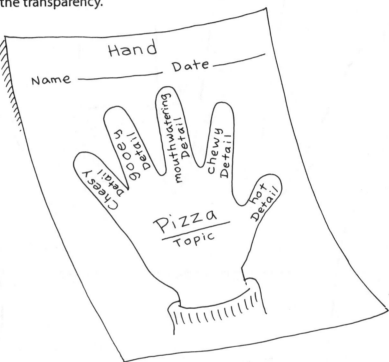

Invite students to choose a Hand, Star, Me, or Sun reproducible, and have students return to their desks and complete Part 1 for a topic of their choice.

Part 2

 For students who are still struggling to write detailed sentences, this same visual can be used to write one long sentence with many detail words.

Display the completed transparency. On chart paper, model how to use a topic word, such as *pizza*, to create a topic sentence, such as *I love pizza.* Read aloud the details, such as *cheesy, gooey, mouthwatering, chewy* and *hot,* and use these words to create detail sentences that support the topic sentence. For example, *Eating pizza is a mouthwatering experience. The toppings are cheesy, hot, and gooey. The crust is so chewy!* End with a sentence that uses the topic word again. Your completed paragraph could read as follows:

> *I love pizza! Eating pizza is a mouthwatering experience. The toppings are cheesy, hot, and gooey. The crust is so chewy! I think I'll go eat pizza now.*

Hand

Name _____   Date _____

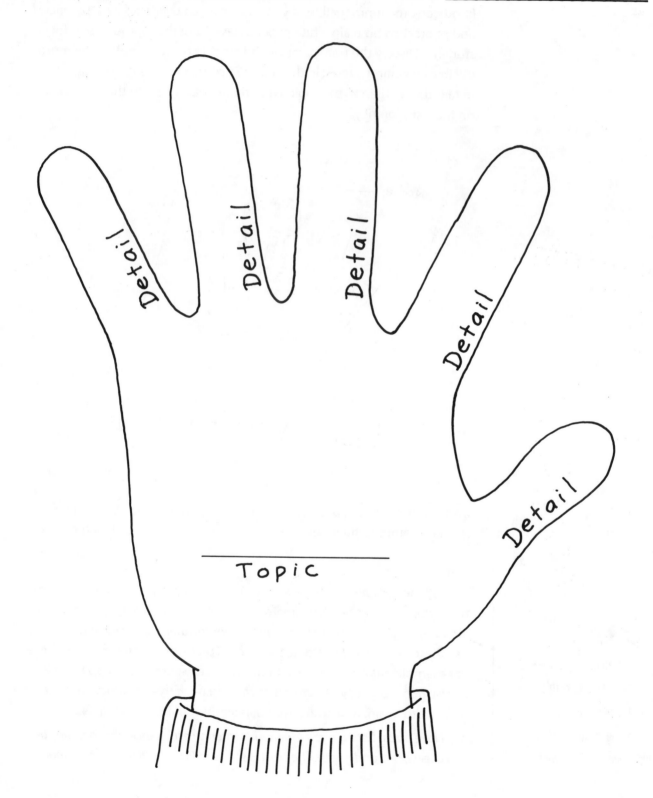

Detail

Detail

Detail

Detail

Detail

Topic

Star

Name _____   Date _____

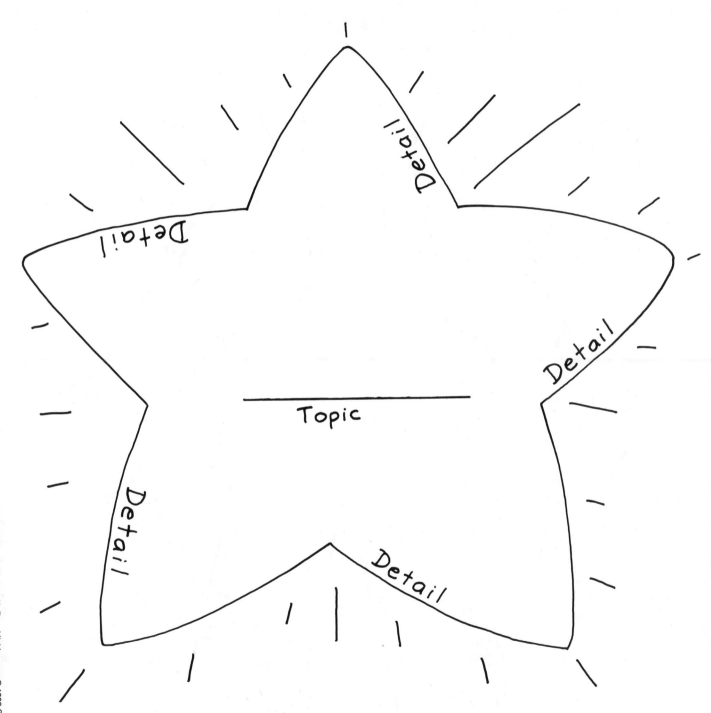

Topic

Detail

Detail

Detail

Detail

Me

Name _____ Date _____

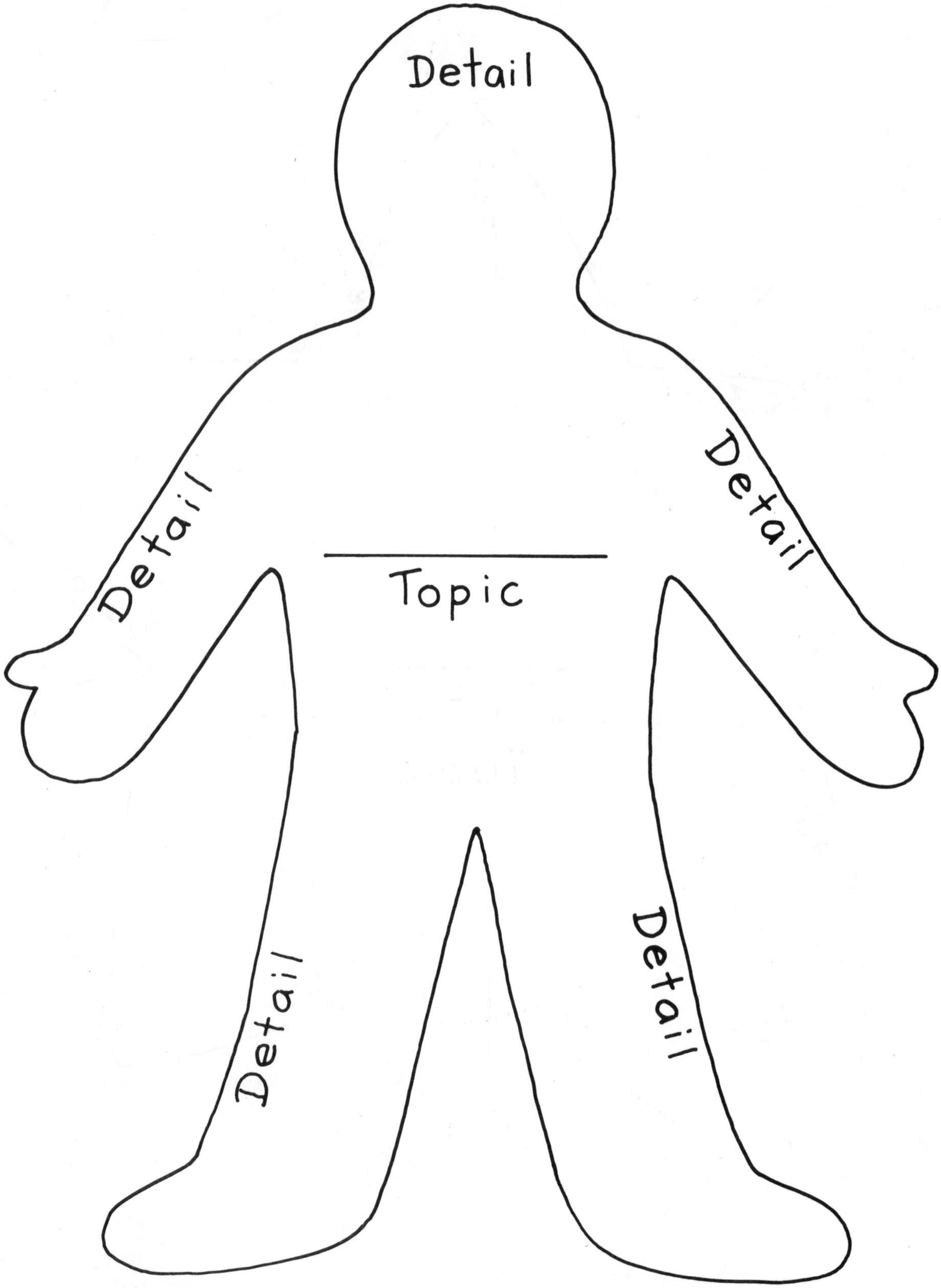

Detail

Detail

Detail

_____
Topic

Detail

Detail

Solving Writing Problems with Easy Mini-Lessons © 1999 Creative Teaching Press

Sun

Name _____ Date _____

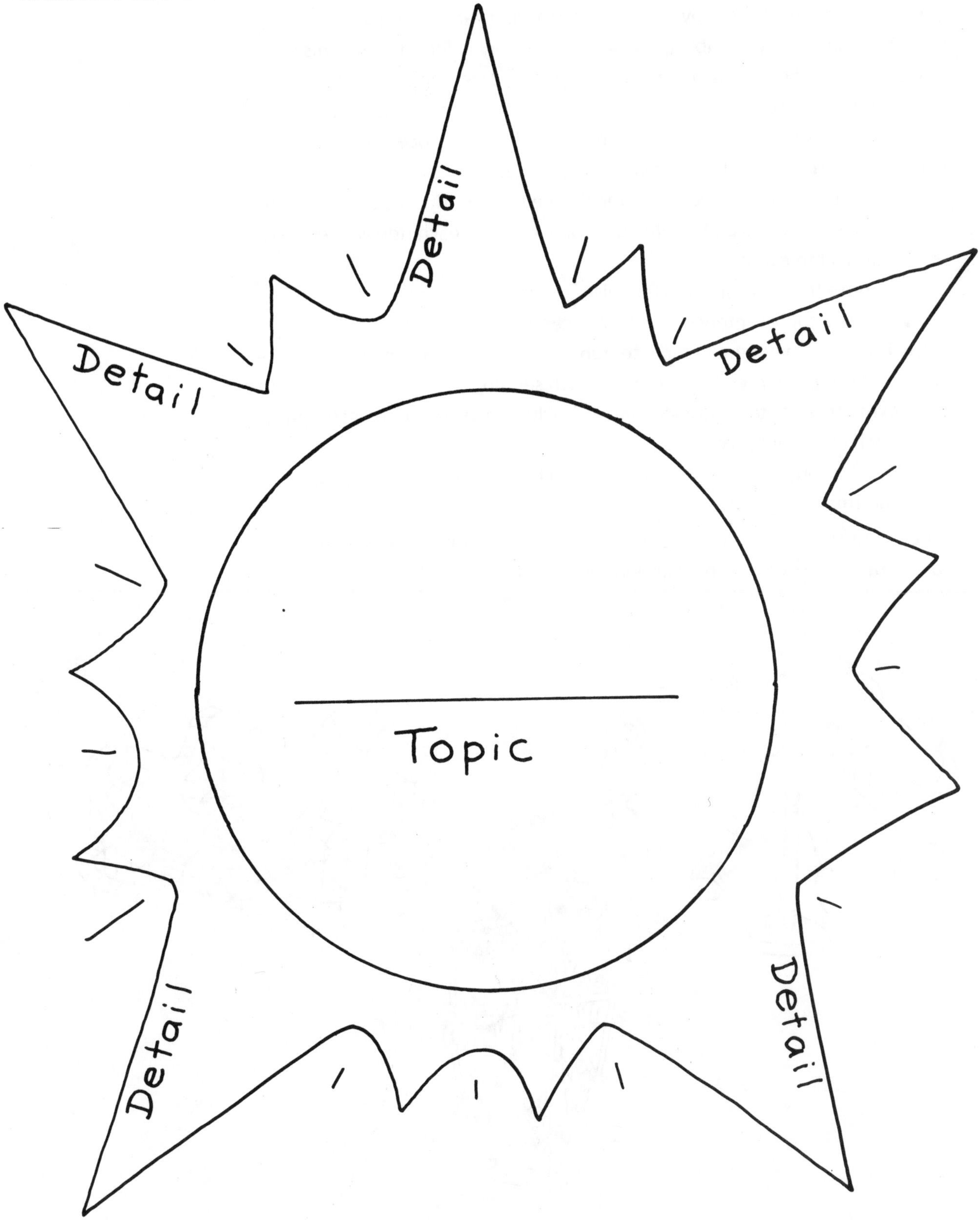

Detail

Detail

Detail

_____

Topic

Detail

Detail

Starting New Paragraphs in an Essay

When students are ready to write a multiparagraph essay, they often write one long paragraph comprised of a list of events and related details. Explain to students that when a writer begins writing about a new topic, a new paragraph begins. Photocopy on an overhead transparency the Starting New Paragraphs reproducible (page 47), and display it. Tell students this is a simple method of brainstorming and writing an essay that helps them know when to start a new paragraph. Read and discuss each step on the transparency. Then model on chart paper the following process, and ask students to help you write about your experience.

- Brainstorm a list of events related to one topic. A trip to an amusement park is an example of an effective topic because each ride is a separate but related event.
- Choose three events out of the list.
- Create a topic sentence that introduces all of the events.
- Turn each event into a topic sentence, writing each on an indented line and skipping three lines between each sentence.
- Write three detail sentences and a concluding sentence to accompany each topic sentence.
- Read through the completed essay to check for flow and missing information.

When your class essay is complete, invite students to follow the same process to compose an essay in their daily writing.

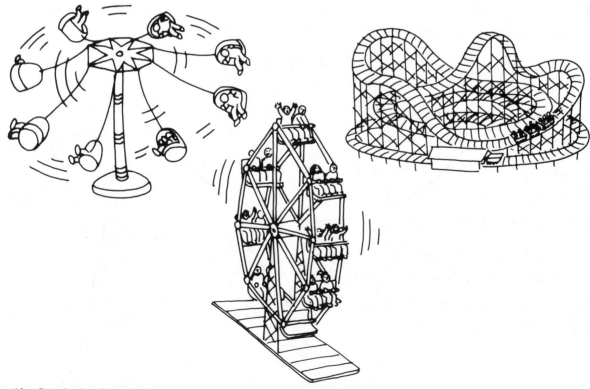

Starting New Paragraphs

1. Make a list of ideas:

On my Colorado vacation . . .
   we ate pancakes every morning.
   ✖ we picked up stones from the creek.
   ✖ my dad built a fire.
   my brother caught a fish.
   ✖ we built a snowman.

2. Decide which ideas you are going to use in your writing and place an ✖ by them.
3. Think of a topic sentence that includes all your ideas. In this case, the author chose *I went to Colorado with my family on vacation.*
4. Each idea becomes the topic sentence of a paragraph. Don't forget to indent to show when a new paragraph begins.
5. Then write detail and concluding sentences to complete the paragraphs.

   I went to Colorado with my family on vacation. My mother, father, brother, and I went. We stayed in a cabin with a fireplace! It snowed every day! The first day was the most fun.

   When we got there, the first thing we did was go looking for some stones in a nearby creek. The stones were bright and shiny. I couldn't believe how smooth they were. We wore high boots to get the stones because the water was very cold. We collected our stones and ran back to the cabin.

   Later, my dad built a fire. He used sticks we gathered in the forest and wood we bought from the store. I didn't know my dad could build a fire. It was very smoky until my dad opened the flue. The fire made my hands toasty warm.

   After lunch, my brother and I built a snowman. We used sticks for his arms and moss for his hair. We found stones and made buttons down his front. My mom took a picture of all of us with the snowman. I had a wonderful time on my vacation in Colorado.

Solving Writing Problems with Easy Mini-Lessons © 1999 Creative Teaching Press

Indenting Paragraphs

Create a transparency of a page from a book that has a mix of dialogue and full paragraphs. Ask students how they can tell when a paragraph starts. Introduce the word *indent,* and write it along the margin of the transparency. Tell students that writers leave space at the beginning of the first line of their paragraphs as a signal to the reader that the topic is changing or a new character is speaking. After you read each paragraph together, encourage volunteers to identify how the topic has changed. Next, display a piece of writing you have created that has at least two paragraphs but no indent or paragraph break. Invite students to read the piece and discuss where the paragraph break would come. When the class has agreed on the correct location for the indent, demonstrate how to use two finger widths to measure the space for the indent. Then encourage students to start each paragraph in their own writing with an indent as they change from one topic to another.

Break It Down Invite students to work in small groups to identify the topic of two or three paragraphs they have chosen from core literature, science texts, or social studies texts.

Catching an Essay in a Web

Model how to complete a graphic organizer such as the Writer's Web reproducible (page 49). Invite students to suggest a topic and details for you to place on the web. In particular, tell students that the main idea in the center of the web becomes the topic sentence for the entire essay and comes first in an introductory paragraph. The four key details are written in the diamonds of the web and become the topic sentence of each of the four paragraphs in the body of the essay. The ovals hold details that support each of those topic sentences. Model how to write the essay and refer to the organizer to make choices about topic sentences, what details to include, and concluding sentences. The concluding paragraph can restate the main idea or end with feelings about the topic, questions, advice, or a meaningful quote. (See page 55 for a mini-lesson on story endings.)

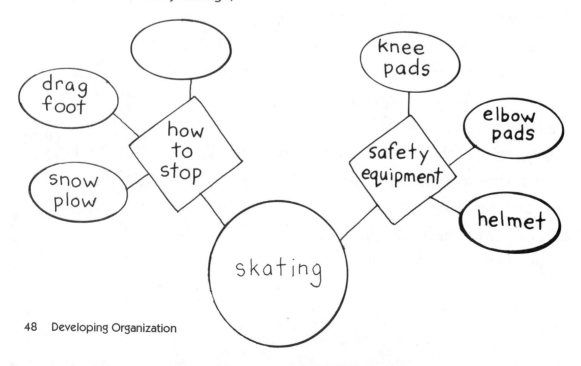

Writer's Web

Name _____   Date _____

Compare-and-Contrast Paragraphs

Display two different attribute blocks, and invite students to tell you ways in which they are alike and different. List their responses on chart or butcher paper under the headings *Alike* and *Different*.

Introduce the words *compare* and *contrast*. Indicate the appropriate column, and tell students that to compare is to tell how two items are alike and to contrast is to tell how two items are different. As a class, write a quick paragraph that tells how the two pattern blocks are alike and different. Underline each word or phrase that compares or contrasts the blocks. Examples of comparing and contrasting words and phrases include *like, as, similar, than, the same, unlike, different, in contrast,* and *differ from.* When the paragraph is complete, invite students to read the underlined vocabulary. Ask students to use these words to write a paragraph that compares and contrasts two objects, people, or places of their choice.

Cause-and-Effect Paragraphs

Photocopy on an overhead transparency the Cause and Effect reproducible (page 51). Demonstrate the meaning of cause and effect by knocking on a desk and listening to the noise. Tell students the cause was the knock and the noise was the effect. Invite them to brainstorm other examples of cause and effect. Then display the Cause and Effect transparency. Invite volunteers to read the paragraph and identify statements of cause and effect. Underline the statements they find, and circle words and phrases that indicate cause and effect, such as *so, since, because, when, made,* and *therefore.* This activity can be repeated with newspaper articles. Invite students to write about a situation involving cause and effect, such as a ball game or playground interaction. Encourage sharing of student writing.

Break It Down Invite students to act out a cause and effect scene before writing about it.

Cause and Effect

This morning my dad woke up late so he was in a hurry. Since he was in a hurry, he ran through the kitchen. My mom yelled, "Henry!" because my dad knocked over the orange juice when he ran into the kitchen table. When my mom yelled, my brother jumped in surprise. I laughed because my brother jumped and this made my mom and dad laugh, therefore everyone was happy. It was a crazy morning because my dad woke up late, but we all ended up laughing.

Solving Writing Problems with Easy Mini-Lessons © 1999 Creative Teaching Press

Hooks

Choose a piece of literature that models a specific type of story opening (see the list below). Read the lead to students, and invite them to discuss how the author pulls the reader into the story. Tell students this beginning is called the hook. Read aloud other examples of story hooks, and have students discuss some of the differences between the different types of story hooks. Encourage students to try some of the following types of hooks in their writing.

Types of Hooks and Examples in Literature

Give a Startling Fact
The Gold Coin by Alma Flor Ada
The True Story of the Three Little Pigs! By A. Wolf by Jon Scieszka
Tuck Triumphant by Theodore Taylor

Describe the Setting
The Black Stallion by Walter Farley
Cloudy With a Chance of Meatballs by Judi Barrett
My Side of the Mountain by Jean Craighead George

Use a Sound
Bridge to Terabithia by Katherine Paterson
Stone Fox by John Reynolds Gardiner
Zeely by Virginia Hamilton

Begin with Dialogue
Arthur's First Sleepover by Marc Brown
The Day Jimmy's Boa Ate the Wash by Trinka Hakes Noble
King Bidgood's in the Bathtub by Audrey Wood

Start with a Question
Charlotte's Web by E. B. White
Chester, the Worldly Pig by Bill Peet

Rewrite a Hook

Read aloud the beginning paragraph of a book students enjoy. Brainstorm different ways the class could change the beginning, and then have students work with a partner to write a new lead for the story. Invite pairs to read the revised leads to the class.

Which Hook Is It?

After students are exposed to the many ways writers begin books, choose books with different leads. Read aloud the first few paragraphs, and ask students to name the type of lead the writer used. Then invite students to choose a style to experiment with in their writing.

Hook the Reader

Photocopy a class set of the Gotcha! reproducible (page 54). Ask students if they have ever been fishing. Ask those who have to talk about baiting a hook to catch a fish. Tell students that a good story beginning is just like going fishing. You throw the beginning out there, a reader reads it, and then the reader decides whether or not to read the rest of the story. Compare an exciting lead to the unique hooks fishermen create. Give each student a Gotcha! reproducible, and invite students to write a short story with a hook that starts with a sound, question, or another unusual beginning. Display completed pieces in the room as a reminder of different ways to start stories.

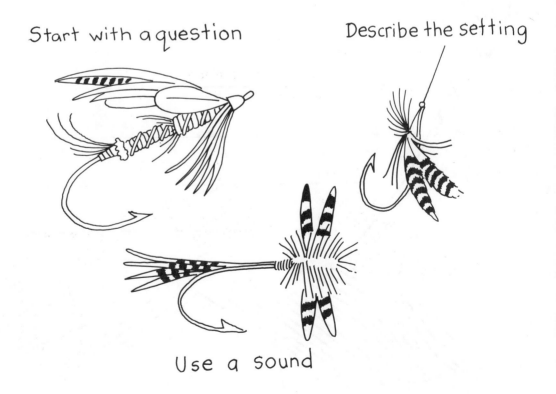

Start with a question

Describe the setting

Use a sound

Gotcha!

Name _____   Date _____

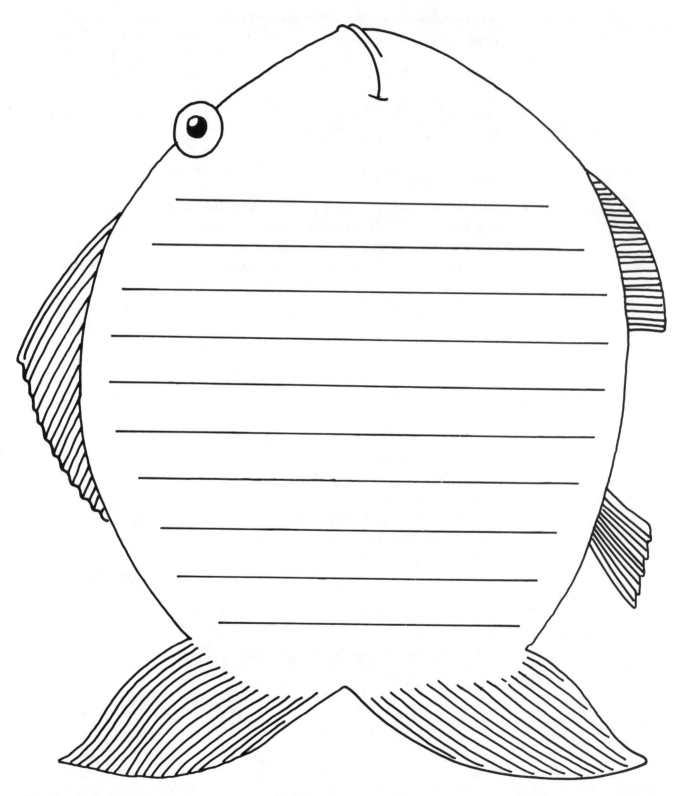

Ways to End a Story

Read aloud a book that demonstrates a specific type of story ending (see the list below). Stop before the last page, and ask students to predict how the story will end. Record their predictions, and then finish the book. Invite students to tell what they liked and disliked about the book's ending, and then tell students the type of ending the author used. Read aloud another book, again stopping before the end. This time, invite students to apply the type of ending they read in the previous book to the new book. Record their ending, finish the book, and invite students to compare their ending to the author's ending. Invite students to apply the type of ending to a piece of their own. Repeat the lesson with new books to expose students to a variety of endings that they can apply to their own writing.

Types of Endings and Examples in Literature

Advise the Reader
How Smudge Came by Nan Gregory
Mike Mulligan and His Steam Shovel by Virginia Lee Burton
To Climb a Waterfall by Jean Craighead George

Reword the Beginning
The Most Obedient Dog in the World by Anita Jeram
My Mama Had a Dancing Heart by Libba Moore Gray
The Secret in the Matchbox by Val Willis

End with a Quote
Amazing Grace by Mary Hoffman
The Boy Who Wouldn't Go to Bed by Helen Cooper
The Rooster's Gift by Pam Conrad

End with a Feeling
I Love You the Purplest by Barbara M. Joosse
The Little Engine that Could by Watty Piper
Peter's Move by Alexander James

End with a Question
Grandpa's Song by Tony Johnston
Shoes from Grandpa by Mem Fox
Which Witch Is Which? by Pat Hutchins

Using Literature to Show Story Organization

The Grouchy Ladybug by Eric Carle
This book demonstrates sequence by displaying the time of each event. Teach a brief lesson on writing time words, and then invite students to include time in their writing to show the order of events.

If You Give a Mouse a Cookie by Laura Joffe Numeroff
In this book, a boy gives a mouse a cookie and unleashes a chain of funny events. Read aloud this story, and focus on how the author organizes the story. Tell students that the return to the beginning is one way that a reader knows the story is over without saying *The End*. Invite students to try this style of ending in their writing.

In the Small, Small Pond by Denise Fleming
This book is full of the vocabulary of sounds. Invite students to list the sounds, and encourage them to choose a sound with which to begin their writing.

Like Jake and Me by Mavis Jukes
In this story, a young boy, Alex, cannot find what he and his stepfather have in common. This changes when Alex saves his stepfather from a fuzzy spider. This book starts out with a detailed description of the setting. Invite students to describe the setting when they begin to write to engage the reader in the story.

The Relatives Came by Cynthia Rylant
In this book, a carload of relatives, so large one cannot be told from another, comes to visit. This book ends in the same place that it began. Use the book to model a circular ending. Invite students to use this style of ending in their writing.

Rosie's Walk by Pat Hutchins
This classic is about an oblivious hen who evades a wolf by leading him into progressively more detrimental situations without ever realizing it. This selection is good for modeling a circular ending. Invite students to use this style of ending in their writing.

The Seashore Book by Charlotte Zolotow
This book uses specific details as it tells of a mother describing the seashore to her son. It starts with a quote as its lead. Invite students to use this style as a way to engage the reader.

Shoes from Grandpa by Mem Fox
Jessie's family tells her lovingly of the clothes they want to give her to go with the shoes she received from Grandpa. This story starts with a question lead. Invite students to begin their writing with a question.

Maintaining Focus

In anything at all, perfection is finally attained, not when there is no longer anything to add, but when there is no longer anything to take away.
—Antoine de
   Saint Exupery

How many times have you looked up from an entertaining piece of student writing, still unsure of your young writer's topic? Young writers struggle with focus because they write as storytellers not as readers; it is difficult for them to distinguish between what is relevant and irrelevant when the topic is their own life. A focused story gives a clear picture of the event and excludes additional, irrelevant information. Teaching your students to focus their writing is also teaching your students to read their own writing as readers, not as writers. This section teaches students how to write a strong topic sentence, defines the meaning of focus, and gives them practice at choosing a focused topic.

Teaching Topic Sentences

Write on chart or butcher paper four lists made of a few events related to one topic.

My Birthday
- opening presents
- eating the cake
- playing musical chairs

Topic Sentence: I had a great birthday!

The Beach
- jumping the waves
- building a sand castle
- collecting shells

Topic sentence: My family and I went to the beach.

First Day of School
- meet our new teacher
- eat in the cafeteria
- see our friends

Topic Sentence:

Read the first two lists, and model how to generate a heading for each list. Invite students to read the next two lists, and have them decide on headings for each one. Explain that authors need to identify the big idea or topic that their details are about. Point out that writers tell their readers what the writing is about in the topic sentence. Tell students the topic sentence is often the first sentence. Model how to write a topic sentence for the first two lists. Invite students to write a topic sentence for lists three and four. When students are comfortable with composing topic sentences, have the class choose a topic, brainstorm details, and create a topic sentence. Finally, encourage students to choose a topic of their own, brainstorm details, and create a topic sentence. If time permits, have students use their brainstormed list to generate detail sen-

Defining Focus

Photocopy the A Clear Topic reproducible (page 59) on an overhead transparency. On the overhead projector, write *focus,* but adjust the lens so that the word is blurry. Ask students to describe your action as you turn the knob and bring the word into focus. When students have described your action as making it clear, explain that focus means to make clear. Suggest that the goal of good writers is to write a focused piece, one that makes the topic clear. Display *The Museum* and *The Dinosaur Exhibit,* and ask students to consider whether the author has chosen a topic sentence that can be described well in just one paragraph. Read aloud the pieces together, comparing and contrasting the two paragraphs. Have students contribute details the author could add to support the topic sentence in each paragraph. Invite students to notice that the topic sentence of *The Dinosaur Exhibit* effectively focuses the writing on just one part of the museum, while the topic sentence of *The Museum* generates enough ideas for pages of writing. Provide students with a topic sentence, and invite them to write a focused paragraph that includes detail sentences that support the topic.

Suggested topic sentences include the following:

- I love pizza!
- My mom is terrific.
- My favorite game is _____.
- My desk is very organized/disorganized.
- Let me tell you how it felt to score the winning goal/touchdown/run.

A Clear Topic

The Museum

This year's field trip was great. Our parent volunteer was nice. We went to the gift shop. Did you see the dinosaur exhibit? I thought it was the best. I had a good time.

The Dinosaur Exhibit

I loved the dinosaur exhibit at the museum. There were models of little dinosaurs that leaped at me and made me jump! I saw bones bigger than my dog and little, pale bones like a bird's. At one station, I pressed the buttons and heard about each of the different dinosaurs. It was the best dinosaur exhibit I have seen.

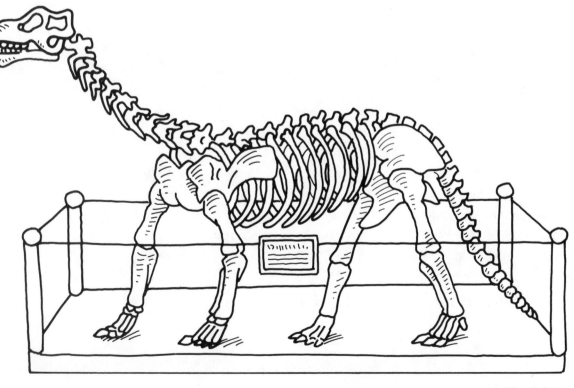

Ready, Set, Go!

Invite students to take a few minutes (choose a time limit appropriate to the writing level of your students) to choose a writing topic. On your signal, have them write as fast as they can about their topic until you tell them to stop. Have students read aloud their writing with a partner and look for off-topic details to weed out. Ask students to write a heading for their topic at the top of their paper. With their partner, students should compare each sentence with the heading to be sure it fits. If a sentence does not match the heading, have students cross it out. When the pairs have edited both partners' papers, have students write a final draft to read to the class.

Tunnel Tubes

Have each student bring a cardboard tube from home. Invite the class to look around the classroom, and then encourage students to look again at the class through their tube. Encourage students to tell what they focused on. Tell students the experience is similar to how writers should think before beginning their writing. Tell them to start with a big topic, like the classroom, and then focus on a specific topic, like the one seen in the tube. Invite students to decorate their "tunnel tube" and then use it to choose a writing topic.

Break It Down Invite your tactile students to collect a small item (focused idea) from nature (broad idea) in their tube (e.g., a flower, a beetle, or a blade of grass). Encourage students to brainstorm words that describe the item and then write a focused paragraph on just that one object or creature.

Frame the Topic

Cut out and color a frame from the Frame the Topic reproducible (page 61). Select a writing sample with several apparent topics, and center the frame on one of those topics. Ask volunteers to provide detail sentences to accompany the framed topic. Give each student a frame. Invite each student to decorate his or her frame and store it in a writing folder. When the class understands how to use the frame, use it as a conferencing tool to help students whose work needs focus.

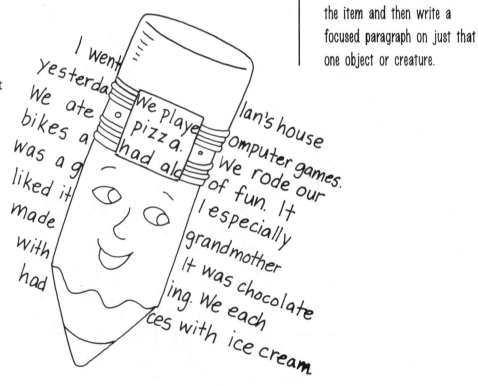

Frame the Topic

cut out square

cut out square

Cut It Up

Write the sample paragraph (below) on chart paper. Invite students to read aloud the paragraph with you. Have them look at each sentence, and ask whether the sentence tells about Becky's party or Becky's kite. Then use scissors to cut apart the sentences. Have students help you sort the sentences. Post the sentences on the board or a clean sheet of chart paper. Arrange the sentences into new paragraphs, and read them aloud with the class. With more fluent writers, discuss the need for a paragraph break when starting a new topic. Encourage students to examine their writing and revise any sections that need a clearer focus.

Sample Paragraph

I was really excited because I was going to Becky's birthday party. Becky's party was a pool party at her grandmother's house. I decided to give her a kite for her birthday. We bought it at the neighborhood store. I got one that has a pretty rainbow on it. Becky's kite has sparkles on it. I had a fun time swimming at the party. The best part was getting to jump off the diving board!

Break It Down Give index cards or sticky notes to a student who goes back and forth between topics in his or her writing. Have the student write a different sentence from the mixed-up paragraph on each card. Then invite the student to sort the cards by topic, and encourage him or her to tell you why each choice was made. When the sorting is complete, help the student reorganize the sentences into a new, focused paragraph for each topic. Students may recognize that they need more details to support a topic or that some information can be cut altogether.

Color-Coded Topics

Photocopy on an overhead transparency the My Grandma and Sasha reproducible (page 64). Read the piece to the class, using a bookmark to direct their eyes as they read silently with you. Invite students to tell you the focus of the piece. Students should identify two distinct topics: my grandmother and my dog. Underline anything that tells about my grandmother in orange and anything that tells about my dog in green. On a new transparency, record the orange sentences and then the green sentences. Discuss with the class the differences between the sentence lists and the original piece. Tell students that the two groups do not belong in the same story. Invite volunteers to help you identify the sentences that can be used to write a focused paragraph about Sasha at the soccer game or the grandmother. Encourage students to examine previous writing and identify places where they may need to clarify the focus by separating one piece into two new ones.

My Grandma and Sasha

Yesterday I went to see my grandmother. I like visiting my grandmother. My dog's name is Sasha. She is tan with brown spots. I took Sasha to my soccer game. My grandmother drove me to my soccer game. She cheered for my team. Sasha kept barking every time my team scored. She was a good dog though; she never ran onto the field. I can take Sasha anywhere. After the game, grandma took my friends and me out to pizza. My grandmother grew up on a farm. She makes my friends lau telling sto:

My Grandma and Sasha

Yesterday I went to see my grandmother. I like visiting my grandmother. My dog's name is Sasha. She is tan with brown spots. I took Sasha to my soccer game. My grandmother drove me to my soccer game. She cheered for my team. Sasha kept barking every time my team scored. She was a good dog though; she never ran onto the field. I can take Sasha anywhere. After the game, grandma took my friends and me out to pizza. My grandmother grew up on a farm. She makes my friends laugh by telling stories from when she was young. I am very proud of her.

Solving Writing Problems with Easy Mini-Lessons © 1999 Creative Teaching Press

Using Literature to Teach Focus

Corduroy by Don Freeman
This classic story about a stuffed bear who loses a button and gains a home is an excellent choice to teach children about focus. After reading the story, discuss the writer's focus on one item, the button, throughout the entire story. Invite students to choose one object for their topic.

The Flower Garden by Eve Bunting
In this book, a girl and her father prepare the mother's birthday garden. Read aloud the story, and invite students to brainstorm all the topics they could focus on in the garden. Encourage students to focus on one item, such as a flower, and describe it with specific details.

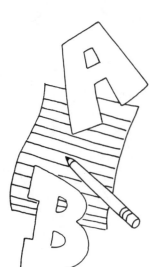

The Important Book by Margaret Wise Brown
This book reveals the important things about everyday objects. Read aloud the book, and invite students to tell you each broad topic and its corresponding "important thing." Encourage students to brainstorm new topics and related important things. Invite students to write about an object.

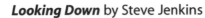

Keep Looking! by Millicent Selsam and Joyce Hunt
An empty house is revealed to be home to different active animals. Invite students to choose one of the animals and write about it.

Looking Down by Steve Jenkins
This is a wordless book that starts in outer space. Each page views Earth more closely. The last few pages reveal a park, and then, finally, a ladybug hiding in the grass. Invite students to discuss their reaction as the author narrowed his focus.

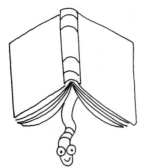

Pug's Hugs by Margaret Allen (Creative Teaching Press)
This story is about a puppy who gets into trouble throughout the day but finally finds one activity that earns praise. Invite students to select an animal in which they are interested and research facts about this animal. Use this opportunity to model how to record facts on a web. Then help students use the web to write a focused paragraph. This book also focuses on the *v, y,* and short *u* phonemes.

Splish, Splash by Margaret Allen (Creative Teaching Press)
This book is about a rabbit who learns to swim. Invite students to tell the story of the rabbit in their own words. This book also focuses on the three-letter blends *str, spl,* and *scr.*

Water by Frank Asch
This is a pattern book that tells all the things water can be. Invite students to count all the ways water is presented in the book. Encourage students to write about an item and all of its uses.

The Way of the Willow Branch by Emery Bernhard
This story follows the journey of a willow branch from the tree to its use as a musical mobile. The writer keeps the focus on the branch. Explain that writers focus on one thing to make it easier for the reader to understand the story. Invite students to write about a day in the life of an object of their choice.

Where's Waldo? by Martin Hanford
Quickly show a small group of children one page of this book, and see if they can find Waldo. After ten seconds, close the book. Invite students to tell the group what they saw. After students share, encourage them to discuss why they were unable to agree on Waldo's location. Compare the lack of visual focus to a lack of written focus. Invite students to draw Waldo by himself and describe him with details.

Improving Description

Life is a big canvas;
throw all the paint
on it you can.
—Danny Kaye

Sometimes it takes a gentle nudge to encourage students to spill forth with the details of their lives. These lessons encourage your students to move beyond the simple, literal telling, to one that brings their writing alive. Clear, specific, vivid descriptions paint a picture in the mind of the reader and are a joy to read. The following mini-lessons teach students how to include effective details through the use of sensory words; color; emotions; similes; metaphors; and the *who, what, where, when,* and *why* of a story.

Adding Description

Write a two-word, noun-verb sentence. Ask students to expand the sentence by adding words. Coach students to contribute describing words before adding more nouns and verbs. An expanded sentence might look like the following:

Dogs barked.

Three dogs barked.

Three brown dogs barked.

Three brown dogs barked loudly.

Three brown dogs barked loudly at a passing car.

Three brown dogs barked loudly at a passing car and woke the neighbors.

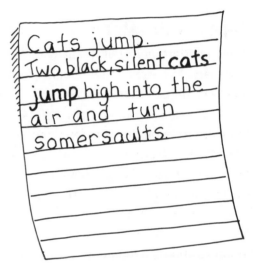

After you have done a few sentences together, invite students to repeat the activity in pairs. You may want to offer noun-verb sentences or invite students to create their own. Have partners read aloud their "before" and "after" sentences.

What Manner of a Monster?

Have each student draw and color a monster on a half sheet of paper. When the drawings are complete, invite students to write a descriptive paragraph about their monster. Emphasize that another student will be using their writing as a guide for drawing the monster. When students have completed their paragraph, have them hide the original illustration and find a partner with whom to trade paragraphs. Invite students to draw the monster described in their partner's writing and then compare the new drawing to the original one. Encourage partners to discuss details missing from the paragraph. Invite students to revise their paragraph to include the missing details, and post the writing and the monsters as a class bulletin board.

Only What It Says

Photocopy The Beach reproducible (page 69) on an overhead transparency, and read it aloud. Have each student draw the scene and then share his or her drawing. Remind students not to add extra details to their drawing. Compare the student's drawings to the story by matching details in the story to details in their drawings. Discuss how students can change their own writing to make it easier for readers to draw or mentally picture what they read. The first time you do this lesson, read the story twice; once while students listen and once while they draw. After students practice, have them do the activity with a partner and each other's writing.

Explode the Moment

Model this activity by using many sensory details to describe a brief moment. For example, describe the thoughts, feelings, sights, sounds, and smells of the five minutes before the bell on the first day of school. Invite students to tell about the same moment from their perspective or to choose a different moment to "explode" with description (e.g., the moment in which everyone yelled *Surprise!* at their birthday party or getting on an exciting ride at an amusement park). Discuss how authors "explode the moment" by filling their writing with sensory details, and tell how students could use each of their senses in describing their moment. Emphasize that this is not a sequential retelling, but a detailed description about a short period of time. Invite students to choose a moment to write about and explode with description. Encourage sharing of completed pieces.

Break It Down Provide each student with a copy of the Explode the Moment reproducible (page 70). Then have students recall and write words that describe a specific moment. Encourage students to notice that we have many more ways to describe what we see and touch than we do for our other senses. Students may benefit from group discussion to brainstorm new ways to describe their sensations of hearing, smelling, and tasting. Invite students to use this brainstormed web to write their finished piece.

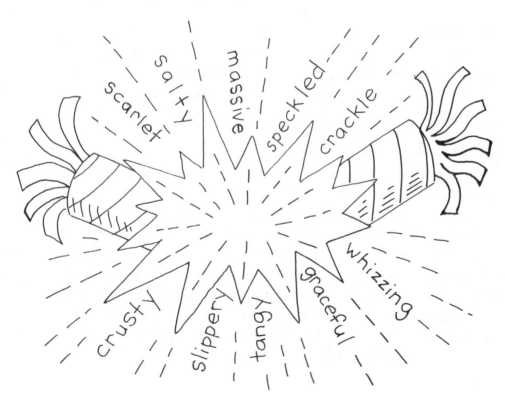

The Beach

It was a perfect day at the beach. The clouds looked like white strokes of paint on a light blue paper sky. My friend Sam and I sat with our legs stretched out on the shore of the speckled gray and white beach. We were quietly watching a large, white pelican that was perched on a huge, black rock next to us. The waves were gentle, and a small crab was burying itself in the wet sand. We never wanted this glorious day to end.

Explode the Moment

Name _____   Date _____

Touching Words

_____
_____
_____
_____

Directions: Write words that describe what you saw, smelled, tasted, heard, or touched.

Seeing Words

_____
_____
_____
_____

Topic

_____
_____
_____

Hearing Words

_____
_____
_____

Smelling Words

_____
_____
_____

Tasting Words

_____
_____
_____

Solving Writing Problems with Easy Mini-Lessons © 1999 Creative Teaching Press

Emotions

Have the class generate a list of emotions for you to record on the chalkboard. Read aloud the completed list, and ask students to raise their hand, without speaking, if they have ever felt that emotion. Respond with comments such as *I see many of us have felt that way.* When you have gone through the list, invite students to tell about times they have had these feelings. Display books and suggest that one way the authors of these books made their stories interesting was by including the emotions of their characters. Encourage students to include feelings in their writing to make the reader think *Oh! I've felt that way, too.* Have students return to previous writing or begin a new topic, and encourage them to include feelings.

Suggested titles to use with this lesson include the following:

Alexander and the Terrible, Horrible, No Good, Very Bad Day by Judith Viorst
A Baby Sister for Frances by Russell Hoban
How to Eat Fried Worms by Thomas Rockwell
Ramona the Pest by Beverly Cleary
Something on My Mind by Nikki Grimes
Stellaluna by Jannell Cannon
The Tenth Good Thing About Barney by Judith Viorst
The Two of Them by Mildred Pitts Walker

Follow this lesson with the Thumbing through the Thesaurus lesson (page 92) so students may add new descriptive words to their vocabulary.

 Have students write the sentence starters *I see, I smell, I hear,* and *I touch.* Give each student a clipboard, and invite students to complete these sentences about their item during the walk.

Walk It Out

Tell students they will be taking a walk and when they return they will write a description of one item. Discuss which senses students will use on their walk. Most students will choose an item they can see, touch, and smell (e.g., leaf, dandelion, chain-link fence, or mailbox) but not taste. Some students will be able to hear and see an animal, but not touch it. After your discussion, take the class for a walk. Encourage students to focus on one item and use their senses to observe that item. When you return to the classroom, have them write down what they observed. Invite sharing of finished pieces.

Vivid Vocabulary

Show students an illustration with beautiful colors and a black and white photocopy of the same page. Invite students to tell about their reactions to both pages, including which page they prefer and why. Then relate their preference for color to their writing by reading the following sets of sentences and inviting students to tell which they prefer and why.

a. The blue and white speckled egg lay in the bright green grass.
b. The egg lay in the grass.

a. The ruby red fireworks exploded in the pitch black sky.
b. The fireworks exploded in the sky.

a. David hugged the puppy.
b. David hugged the black and brown spotted puppy.

Encourage students to read their previous writing and add color words.

Break It Down Write the example sentences on an overhead transparency so students can read along with you. Add three sample sentences, and invite students to improve them by adding words that describe the color.

Magic Number Three

Have the class pick a topic for you to write about. Then invite volunteers to contribute three details they want you to tell them about the topic. (An example is provided below.) Compose a short paragraph that addresses the three details while students watch. Talk your way through the piece so that students benefit from hearing you think aloud. Invite the class to read the finished piece. Ask volunteers to find the three details. As an alternative to quiet writing, consider having small groups brainstorm a topic and three details about that topic. Distribute chart paper to each group, and ask the groups to write complete paragraphs to post around the room.

Topic: Skate Night

Details
1. Who goes to Skate Night?
2. When is Skate Night?
3. Why do I go to Skate Night?

Once a month I go to Skate Night. It takes place on the first Thursday of every

Piggyback Sentences

Ask students to describe what it means to give someone a piggyback ride. Tell students that piggyback sentences give the first sentence a lift by adding more detail for the reader. Write a simple topic sentence on a sentence strip, and invite a volunteer to hold it. Encourage the class to develop a detail sentence to accompany the topic sentence. Write this new detail sentence on another sentence strip, and have a volunteer hold it. Reread the two sentences, and ask the class for a third sentence. Continue in this manner until you have something like the following example:

Pizza tastes good.
Pizza tastes good. The cheese is really gooey and the sauce has lots of spices.
Pizza tastes good. The cheese is really gooey and the sauce has lots of spices. I like when the crust is buttery and chewy.

Invite students to compare the new simple paragraph with the solitary sentence. Repeat the activity with new topic sentences such as *I went to the park,* *The beach was exciting,* or *I like to go to the zoo.* When students understand how to add new detail sentences to the topic sentence, give them two topic sentences to develop independently.

Can You Picture That?

Display a book that has pictures that tell the story, such as *How Much Is That Doggie in the Window* by Iza Trapani. Open the book to any page, holding it so the class can see the page but you cannot. Ask the class questions about the picture. Use the following questions as examples.

Q: What characters are on this page?
A: There are two characters. One is a girl and one is a boy.

Q: What is the girl doing?
A: She is tying her shoe.

Q: How old is she?
A: She's young. I don't think she's old enough to go to school yet.

Q: Is she old enough to walk?
A: Yes.

Finally, attempt to describe the characters and what they are doing. If you are incorrect, have the class offer more information. Repeat the activity with student volunteers. Then invite students to choose a favorite illustration from a book and describe it on paper. Encourage students to have a friend read the paper and guess the content of the illustration. If the partner cannot guess the picture, the student should add more description.

Riddle Groups

Have each student describe an object in the classroom without naming it. Invite students to read their description, and encourage the class to guess what they are describing. Discuss what made some riddles easy and some hard. Refer to examples of excellent descriptions. Encourage students to include additional description in their writing to help the reader see the same item they are describing without having to repeat its name.

Sherlock Holmes

Have groups of students write a brief description of common household items. Label each clue with the number or name of the group, not the author, and collect the clues. Then do the following with each clue:

1. Read the clue to the class.
2. If enough description has been provided for you to guess the identity of the object, the group gets a point.
3. If you cannot guess, the clue is put aside for editing.

After all the clues have been read once, the group provides the answer for clues the teacher did not correctly identify. Then have the class add more description to the clue. Discuss the best clues and what made them work well. Invite students to return to their desks and add details to items in their previous writing. You may wish to model a few clues before having the class begin the activity.

 This same activity can be used to build students' awareness of how authors answer the "W" questions in a chapter book they are reading. Divide the class into small groups, and assign each group a different "W" question. Have groups brainstorm their questions at the start of each chapter to build background or at the close of each chapter to quiz each other for comprehension.

Literature and the "W" Words

Display the cover of a book, such as *Mufaro's Beautiful Daughters* by John Steptoe, that has a detailed illustration that reveals a portion of the content of the book. Invite students to generate a list of questions that ask *who, what, where, when,* and *why* about the various characters and events pictured on the cover of the book. Read through the book, inviting students to raise their hands when they learn the answer to one of their "W" questions. Fairy tales and fables work well for this activity. Discuss with the class how empty the stories would be without answers to these questions. Follow the same procedure as above, and discuss what it is like to be the reader with unanswered questions. Encourage students to answer all the reader's "W" questions in their own writing.

Adjectives

Explain to students that an adjective is a word that describes a noun. Then display an object, and ask students to help you list adjectives. Next, display a few basic noun-verb sentences (e.g., *Monkeys throw, Ants carry, Clowns pedal, Girls laugh*). Have students improve each sentence by having them add adjectives to tell more about the nouns. Finally, encourage students to add adjectives to their previous writing.

"W" Words for the Visiting Speaker

After inviting a speaker to visit your classroom, ask students to pretend they are reporters. Have them generate a list of questions to ask the speaker. Write each question on a sentence strip, and organize the questions by the five "W" words (*who, what, where, when,* and *why*). When the list is complete, tell students these key words are the kinds of questions reporters try to answer about their subject. When the speaker arrives, ask him or her to address these questions while talking to the class, and encourage students to make note of the answers. After the speaker leaves, review the questions and answers with the class. When the class has reviewed the answers to their questions, have students individually write about the speaker.

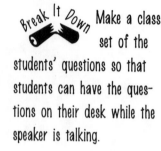 *Break It Down* Make a class set of the students' questions so that students can have the questions on their desk while the speaker is talking.

Simile Wind Sock

Define a simile as a comparison using *like* or *as*. Read a few examples from a book such as *The Unicorn of the West* by Alma Flor Ada. Divide the class into small groups, and provide each group with a book that has several similes in it. Encourage students to look through the books and find similes. Encourage each group to share what they find. Invite groups to make a wind sock by having them write their similes on long strips of paper decorated with borders. Then have students write the title of their book on a large piece of colorfully decorated construction paper and glue the ends together to form a tube. Have students glue the strips so they hang from the bottom of the tube. Hang the Simile Wind Socks from the ceiling.

Suggested titles to use with this lesson include the following:

Everyone Knows What a Dragon Looks Like by Jay Williams
New Shoes for Silvia by Johanna Hurwitz
The Princess Who Lost Her Hair by Tololwa Mollel
Quick As a Cricket by Audrey Wood
Sky Tree: Seeing Science through Art by Thomas Locker
What a Wonderful Day to Be a Cow by Carolyn Lesser

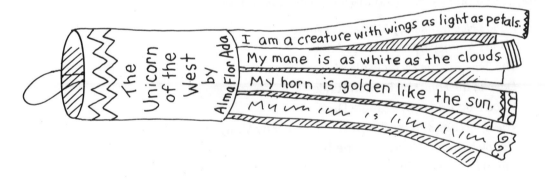

Meet a Metaphor

Define a metaphor as a comparison of two nouns; it is like a simile except it does not use *like* or *as*. Then model writing metaphors by inviting students to suggest an item and encouraging them to brainstorm something to which it can be compared. Write both words on the board or chart paper. Talking aloud, tell how the two are related, use the two in a metaphor, and then write this metaphor beneath both words (e.g., *The tree was an umbrella sheltering us from the blazing sun* or *The lizard was a dart flying from rock to rock*). Continue to provide this whole class practice, then invite volunteers to create their own, before having students create metaphors in small groups. After the small groups have read aloud their contributions to the class, encourage each student to write a paragraph that describes a favorite person, place, or thing. Invite sharing of completed pieces. Alternatively, share some examples with students from literature, such as *The Pumpkin Blanket* by Deborah Turney Zagwyn, before you model how to write metaphors.

Tell the Story

Part 1

Display a wordless book, and have students silently watch while you turn the pages. When you have "read" the story once, ask students what happened in the story. Go through the book again, encouraging students to describe each page. Invite students to use specific details. Record students' descriptions without editing their input.

Part 2

Invite the class to rewrite the unedited descriptions from Part I into complete sentences, having them pay attention to written conventions and word choice. Continue page by page and refer back to the illustrations whenever the class recognizes a need for more description. Record the new complete sentences on clean chart or butcher paper. A longer book can be divided into sections, given to small groups, and reassembled at the end of a writing period for a complete story. Invite volunteers to create illustrations to accompany your new class book. Bind and laminate the book for students to read during quiet reading.

Suggested titles to use with this lesson include the following:

Anno's Flea Market by Mitsumasa Anno
Anno's Journey by Mitsumasa Anno
The Bear and the Fly by Paula Winter
Deep in the Forest by Brinton Turkle
Good Dog, Carl by Alexandra Day
The Grey Lady and the Strawberry Snatcher by Molly Bang
Happy Birthday, Max! by Hanne Turk
Moonlight by Jan Ormerod
Peter Spier's Rain by Peter Spier
Sunshine by Jan Ormerod

 **Break It Down** Invite students to write a general topic in the center of a web and draw details that connect to the topic. Then guide students through developing the web into a paragraph.

Personalize It!

Use an event the entire class has experienced, such as a holiday or a field trip, to model how to personalize a topic. An example might be changing *This weekend it rained hard* to *This weekend, while it was raining, I watched two foot-ball games and ate popcorn with my family*. Have small groups generate a personalized way of rewriting sentences you give them. Finally, have students look for and rewrite their own sentences to provide more interest.

What Did She Say?

Photocopy on an overhead transparency the What Did She Say? reproducible (page 80), and invite volunteers to read the two paragraphs to the class. Encourage students to respond to the following questions:

- Which paragraph gives you the feeling that you are actually there or feels more like real life?
- Which paragraph reveals more about the characters?
- How does dialogue improve the writing?
- What conventions signal the reader that people are talking?

Invite students to suggest a situation for the class to develop. Through discussion, encourage students to create a simple paragraph that you write on chart paper or an overhead transparency. Then discuss how the situation could be developed as dialogue by identifying each character and what he or she could say. When the class has completed the dialogue, invite students to work in pairs to write a brief piece in which the characters talk to each other. Encourage students to write their story idea in a paragraph before beginning to write the dialogue.

What Did She Say?

Paragraph 1

The other day I was riding my bike and saw an old friend of mine. We hadn't seen each other in a long time since we don't live in the same neighborhood anymore. We used to be best friends, but I have a new best friend now.

Paragraph 2

"Katie?" asked a girl with long brown hair and glasses. I had just passed her, so I stopped in surprise. I didn't think I knew this girl, but when I turned around, I screamed!

"Becca! Oh, wow! I can't believe it's you. Your hair has really grown!" I think I was probably blushing. I should have known her; she didn't look all that different. "It's been a really long time." I finished, hoping she would say something.

"Yeah, I guess it has." Becca was smiling. "Want to come over and play? I'm staying with my aunt for the weekend." She pointed to the house on the corner. Her aunt waved at us from the porch. I waved back.

"I have to go," I said, truthfully. "I'm supposed to sleep over at Julie's house tonight, but call me the next time you visit."

"OK," she replied. Then we said together, "Maybe another time." We laughed, said "good-bye," and I waved as I pedaled away.

Solving Writing Problems with Easy Mini-Lessons © 1999 Creative Teaching Press

Using Literature to Develop Description

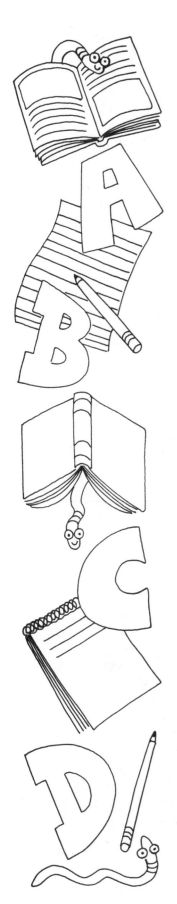

Barn Dance! by Bill Martin Jr.
The author describes the fun in the barn through sound and rhyming words to engage the reader. Explain to the children that describing sensory details, such as smells, textures, colors, sounds, shapes, and sizes, helps readers picture what is happening. Invite students to use sensory details in their writing.

Going to Sleep on the Farm by Wendy Cheyette Lewison
In this book, each animal in the barnyard prepares for sleep. Read this book to students without showing them the illustrations. Then read it again, and show the pictures. Discuss with the students if the pictures they created in their minds matched the ones in the illustrations.

Jo Jo in Outer Space by Margaret Allen (Creative Teaching Press)
Jo Jo is a beaver who finds a new friend in space. Have students look for words that describe size, color, and feelings. This book also focuses on simple word endings such as *-er, -ed, -ly,* and *-y.*

Miss Tizzy by Libba Moore Gray
The children in the neighborhood rally around their beloved Miss Tizzy when she falls ill in this story. Read aloud the story without showing the pictures. Then have students draw what they think Miss Tizzy looks like. Invite students to share their drawings, and then show the pictures in the book. Invite students to tell which details directed their drawings. On the back of each picture, have students write phrases from the story that inspired details in their picture.

My Great Aunt Arizona by Gloria Houston
In this story, a teacher tells the children about places they can travel. She has never been to any of the places, but she tells her class about each place with clear and specific details. Invite students to use description to tell of a place they enjoy.

New Shoes for Silvia by Johanna Hurwitz
This is a story about a girl who receives a new pair of red shoes that are too big. Read aloud the story, and have students list the ways the same pair of shoes is described. This book can also be used to have students identify similes.

Otter On His Own by Doe Boyle
This is the story of a sea otter. Read aloud the book page by page, and ask students to visualize each scene. Encourage them to tell what they are picturing, and then show them the picture.

Out to Gumball Pond by Margaret Allen (Creative Teaching Press)
In this story, a family and their cat run into trouble while looking for their favorite swimming hole. Have students look for words that describe size, color, and feelings. This book also focuses on the following phonemes: *ew; ow* as in *out,* and *ow* as in *now.*

The Polar Express by Chris Van Allsburg
This Christmas story tells of a boy who meets Santa Claus and receives a gift. By the end of the story, students will feel chilly because the author uses such clear details. This is a great book for reviewing *who, what, where, when,* and *why* questions.

Quick As a Cricket by Audrey Wood
A boy joyously tells of himself in this fun story. This book is full of similes. Make a list of the similes students heard. Then have them create their own similes. Invite students to add an illustration, and display student work on a bulletin board.

Rain Talk by Mary Serfozo
A girl and her dog listen to the rain. The author uses sound words to describe all of the different ways rain can sound. Invite students to listen and describe what they hear.

The Seashore Book by Charlotte Zolotow
Read this book about a mother who describes the seashore to her son, and talk about the mother's word choice. Make a list of students' favorite describing words from the book. Invite students to use these words in their writing.

Snowballs by Lois Ehlert
This story is about a variety of snowmen. After you read it aloud, ask students to tell you about their favorite snowmen. Invite them to draw their own snowmen and then describe them in their writing.

Something on My Mind by Nikki Grimes
This book is a collection of poems and illustrations about the thoughts, hopes, joys, and fears of growing up. Invite students to list feeling words and include them in their writing.

The Whales' Song by Dyan Sheldon
In this story, Lilly's grandmother tells of waiting for the whales as a child. Read aloud the book, pausing to talk about the descriptive words the writer uses. Invite students to use some of the new descriptive words in their writing.

Enhancing Word Choice

Do not the most moving
moments of our lives
find us without words?
—Marcel Marceau

 Invite pairs to find examples of "Wow!" words in a favorite book and then write new sentences using these words.

Before you see *very*, *went*, *fun*, *said* and *nice*—your students' comfort words—try a few of the lessons from this section. To teach students the power of words, we must first expand their vocabulary and then encourage them to use it. The mini-lessons in this section teach your students how to find new words and practice using these words effectively. In addition to replacing overused words, the lessons focus on the language of transitions and sequencing.

"Wow!" Words

Display examples of sentence pairs in which one sentence uses common words and the other descriptive words. Read the sentences to students, and have them tell you which sentence they prefer and why. After you have discussed several sentences, invite students to work in pairs to improve sentences you provide. Invite sharing of the new sentences. Display sentence pairs such as the following:

The dog barked.
The black and white beagle howled at the passing car.

The cake was good.
Joan's chocolate birthday cake was mouthwatering.

We went to the park.
My family piled into our van and drove to Taylor Park.

Concrete Colors

Display a large box of crayons, and give a volunteer a red crayon. Invite another student to choose a crayon in a different shade of red. Have volunteers choose other shades of red, and record the name of each crayon on a chart. Have each volunteer scribble next to his or her crayon's name to show the exact shade of red. When most of the red crayons have been selected, have students look at the names of the crayons on the list and discuss what they have in common (i.e., they often compare the red to a commonly known object). Invite students to discuss which of these reds might be the color of a car, clothing, or a house (i.e., *She bought a new pair of brick red jeans*). Invite students to write a paragraph that describes an object with specific color vocabulary.

Wimpy Words

Photocopy on overhead transparencies the Wimpy Words and Worthy Words reproducibles (pages 85 and 86), and display the Wimpy Words transparency. Read aloud the piece once, and then have volunteers reread it and look for the overused words *went* and *very*. Tell students these are "wimpy" words and, because they are overused, students should replace them with stronger, more specific words. Have students brainstorm a list of replacement words. Display the Worthy Words transparency, and have volunteers choose a word from the list to fill in each blank. Encourage students to be on the lookout for other wimpy words they might find in their own writing. Discourage them from replacing wimpy words with slang words such as *awesome* or *cool*.

Repeat this activity with student writing as you see other wimpy words being overused by students. A list of suggested replacement words is provided on the Replacing Overused Words reproducible (page 90).

 Conference with students who use simple vocabulary. Invite them to underline overused words in color, and then replace these words using the class list.

Wimpy Words

It was very hot this weekend. We were very, very hot, too, so we went outdoors. We went in the sprinkler. The sprinkler was very cold. We got very wet. The ice-cream man went down our street, so we went out to meet him. Our ice-cream man is very kind. He waited while we went inside to get money. Our mom was very mad because we went inside with wet feet, but she was very forgiving and gave us money for ice cream anyway. The ice cream was very, very, very delicious!

Worthy Words

It was _____ this weekend. We were _____,
too, so we _____ outdoors. We _____ in the
sprinkler. The sprinkler was _____. We got _____.
The ice-cream man _____ down our street, so we
_____ out to meet him. Our ice-cream man is
_____. He waited while we _____ inside to get
money. Our mom was _____ because we _____
inside with wet feet, but she was _____ and gave us
money for ice cream anyway. The ice cream was
_____!

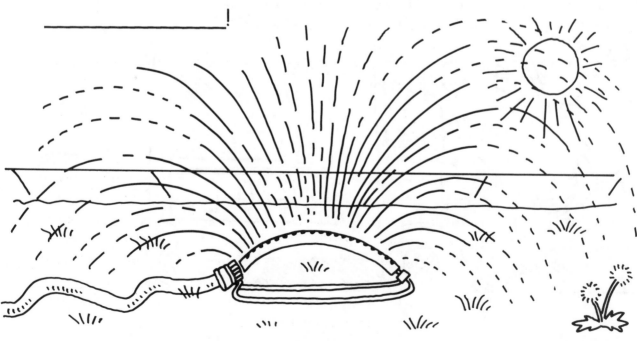

Solving Writing Problems with Easy Mini-Lessons © 1999 Creative Teaching Press

Delicious, Delectable, and Delightful

Display foods your class enjoys, and invite students to tell you how each one tastes. Students will often say the foods taste good. Ask students if the foods all taste good in the same way. Invite students to compare and contrast the tastes of the foods. Write a list of the different describing words students generate for each food. Display this new vocabulary list or add these words to a word wall. Invite students to write about an imaginary meal with their new descriptive words.

Be Specific

Display the sentences below, and invite students to replace general words and phrases, such as *store, shoes, dolls,* and *out to eat,* with specific names and brands. Tell students that writers use specific names and brands to help the reader identify with the writer and to make the scene seem more real.

- We went to the store to buy a new pair of shoes.
- My sister likes to play with dolls.
- We went out to eat with my grandma.
- The other day we went to see a movie.

Encourage students to replace general words or phrases in their writing with specific terms or nouns.

Too Much Fun!

Cut sentence strips in thirds, and write a synonym for *fun* on each one. Display these at the front of the class. Ask students how these synonyms are different. Explain to students that *fun* is often meaningful to a writer, but not specific enough for the reader. Replacing it with words such as *hilarious, exciting,* or *interesting* tells the reader exactly what is meant. Invite volunteers to come to the front of the class, choose the synonym that describes a fun experience, and tell about the experience without using *fun.* Invite students to use specific vocabulary to write about a time they had fun. Synonyms for *fun* include *enjoyable, fantastic, incredible, joyous, marvelous, splendid, terrific,* and *wonderful.*

Sequencing Words

Photocopy on an overhead transparency the Then What? reproducible (page 89), and read aloud the story. Invite students to contribute suggestions to improve the writing. When students suggest that the author has used *then* too frequently, cross out every use of *then* and reread the story. Explain to students that without the *then* in each sentence, it is not possible to know the order in which the events occur. Invite students to brainstorm other words or ways the author could use to show the order, and record their answers on chart or butcher paper. Examples might include

- first, second, third
- first, next, then, last
- before … after
- afterwards
- later
- after a while
- by and by
- later on
- subsequently
- finally
- lastly
- at long last

Add to the list as needed. Then return to the Then What? transparency, and invite volunteers to use words or phrases from the list to improve the paragraph. When this activity is complete, tell students that words that show order of events are called sequencing words. Post the list, and invite students to refer to it during their daily writing. Review these words and phrases after a classroom project such as making a hand puppet. Have students use sequencing words to show the order of how they made the puppet.

Then What?

Our family drove to the beach early on Saturday morning. Then we found a spot to put our things. Then we raced out to jump the waves. Then we built a huge, gray sandcastle. Then we ate our picnic lunch. Then we took a walk and looked for shells. Then we swam in the ocean again. Then we showered off and ran back to the car. Then we drove home, tired from our day at the beach.

Solving Writing Problems with Easy Mini-Lessons © 1999 Creative Teaching Press

Replacing Overused Words

Refer to this list when you want to replace an overused word with a specific, interesting one.

make: build, construct, erect, manufacture, assemble, concoct, devise, produce, form, fashion, create, originate, invent

said: told, stated, claimed, declared, mentioned, referred, remarked, recited, announced, notified, gossiped, whispered, yelled, hollered, hissed, spoke, lectured, gabbed

see: note, notice, observe, perceive, distinguish, discover, discern, detect, spot, behold, regard, picture

go: advance, move, continue, leave, travel, depart, proceed, pass, progress, budge, stir

do: perform, finish, complete, enact, act, achieve, commit, execute, effect, perpetrate

lots: many, numerous, plentiful, countless, various, bountiful, innumerable, abundant, profuse

great: noble, exalted, mighty, notable, distinguished, eminent

got: received, earned, won, acquired, obtained, gathered, retrieved

fine: superior, excellent, splendid, superb, terrific

every: common, familiar, frequent, regular, routine

nice: courteous, friendly, kind, pleasant, amiable, cordial; see also **good**

fun: enjoyable, exciting, fantastic, wonderful, marvelous, joyous, terrific, splendid, incredible

very: incredibly, fantastically, wonderfully, marvelously, extraordinarily, extremely, quite

good: satisfactory, adequate, alright, acceptable, valid, useful; see also **nice**

then: Use sequencing words and phrases such as first, second, third; first, next, then, last; before, after; afterwards; later; after a while; by and by; later on; subsequently; finally; lastly; at long last

Solving Writing Problems with Easy Mini-Lessons © 1999 Creative Teaching Press

 **Break It Down** With a small group, take one overused word, and discuss the slight differences in meaning between its synonyms. For example, synonyms for *walk* would include *stroll* and *hike*. Invite students to demonstrate the differences through pantomime to make the meanings more memorable. Then have students use at least three of the synonyms for that word in a short paragraph.

Synonyms

Tell students that synonyms are words that have similar meanings. Invite students to brainstorm a list of synonyms for *said,* such as *replied, stated,* and *answered.* Record the list on chart or butcher paper. Have student pairs search in favorite texts for synonyms to overused words such as *walked, bad, little, big, funny, happy, pretty, soft, mad,* and *tired.* Invite students to look for these words in their writing, and encourage them to use less-common synonyms instead.

Dressing Up a Favorite Book

Make a transparency of a section of a story with controlled vocabulary or a favorite book with simple text. Ask students to improve the story by having them replace common words with interesting words from their thesaurus or word lists and add description. Invite students to then write on a topic of their choice and edit for word choice and description before sharing with the class.

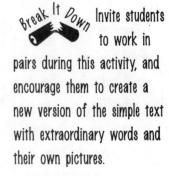

Break It Down Invite students to work in pairs during this activity, and encourage them to create a new version of the simple text with extraordinary words and their own pictures.

Thumbing through the Thesaurus

Photocopy a class set of the Synonym Search reproducible (page 93). Introduce the thesaurus to your students by displaying the book and telling them that it is used to find words that are similar in meaning. Invite students to suggest words for you to locate. Read aloud guide words, and model how to use them to locate the correct page. Read the synonyms for the word. Then ask students to create a sentence that has one of the suggested words. Model how to choose a word that will fit the same sentence. Say the sentence aloud, replacing the old word with its synonym and deciding if the new sentence makes sense. Invite volunteers to take your place, and have them accept new words in context to find in the thesaurus. Then have students work in pairs to practice using the thesaurus by having them complete the Synonym Search reproducible. Review it together. Encourage students to use the thesaurus to find new words to replace overused words in their own writing.

Synonym Search

Name _____   Date _____

Part 1: Next to each word, write the guide words found at the top of the page in your thesaurus.

crash _____   help_____

rare_____   confess _____

reply _____   prize_____

Part 2: Write at least two synonyms for each word and the thesaurus page number where you found the word.

	Synonym	Synonym	Page Number
1. people	_____	_____	_____
2. jump	_____	_____	_____
3. win	_____	_____	_____
4. noise	_____	_____	_____
5. say	_____	_____	_____
6. want	_____	_____	_____
7. friend	_____	_____	_____
8. try	_____	_____	_____
9. stop	_____	_____	_____
10. move	_____	_____	_____
11. different	_____	_____	_____
12. play	_____	_____	_____

Alliteration

Tell students that an alliteration is when a series of words begin with the same sound. Create alliterative phrases using names of students, and ask them to repeat the alliteration back to you. For example, *Rebecca's rainbows are remarkable.* Encourage students to use alliteration to describe an object with which they are familiar and tell the alliterative description to a partner. Invite students to use alliteration in their own writing on a topic of their choice.

Listen Up

Encourage students to sit quietly for one minute and listen for the sounds around them. After the minute has passed, have students name the sounds they heard. Invite students to name sounds heard at the beach, a football game, and a grocery store. Read aloud examples of poems or books that use sounds. Encourage students to add sounds to their writing. You might also consider recording the sounds of various locations as you visit them until you have a library of sounds. Consider recording at places such as the beach, the mall, a movie theatre before the movie begins, or the public library.

Suggested titles to use with this lesson include the following:

Barn Dance! by Bill Martin
In the Small, Small Pond by Denise Fleming
Night Noises by Mem Fox
Rain Drop Splash by Alvin Tresselt
Ride a Purple Pelican by Jack Prelutsky
Where the Sidewalk Ends by Shel Silverstein

Sounds!

Class
footsteps in the hall
door closing
loudspeaker announcement

Beach
waves crashing on the sand
children laughing
seagulls crying

Game
people cheering
players grunting
ball smacking into a hand

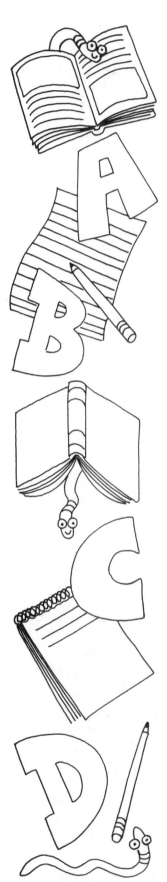

Using Literature to Teach Word Choice

Box Turtle at Long Pond by William T. George
This book models word choice while telling of a day in the life of a box turtle. After reading each page, ask students to identify words that grabbed their attention. List those words, and invite students to use them in their writing.

The Country Bunny and the Little Gold Shoes by DuBose Heyward
A mother bunny is chosen to fill one of five Easter Bunny positions. This book models colorful, descriptive vocabulary. Have the class list new words they heard in the story. Invite students to choose a favorite passage from the story to rewrite in their own words, using new descriptive vocabulary.

I Spy by Margaret Allen (Creative Teaching Press)
In this book a girl who is playing detective sees trouble between a cat and a rat. Invite each student to use a thesaurus to find synonyms for the word *spy* as it is used in this book. Encourage students to retell the story and replace the word *spy* with the new vocabulary. Invite students to draw illustrations to accompany their new book. This book also focuses on the *m, t, f, h, c, r, s,* and short *a* phonemes.

In the Small, Small Pond by Denise Fleming
This book uses sounds to tell the story of animals and insects that live on and in a freshwater pond. After students listen to this story, encourage them to add sound words to their writing.

Lizard in the Sun by Joanne Ryder
This book uses descriptive words to tell of a child who transforms into a lizard for a day. Invite students to identify which words create the mood of the story. Encourage students to use these words in their writing.

Mrs. Rose's Garden by Elaine Greenstein
In this book Mrs. Rose's heart proves as big as her vegetables when she finds a way to share her luck with her neighbors. As you are reading, show students the sequencing words and phrases found in the book such as *every year, one spring, a few weeks later, during, that night, suddenly,* and *in the morning.* Invite students to tell of a time they showed good sportsmanship or secretly helped out another person.

The Napping House by Audrey Wood
This classic book models effective word choice through the use of synonyms for the word *sleeping*. Invite the class to find all the synonyms for *sleeping* and use them in a class poem.

Night Noises by Mem Fox
This book employs sound words throughout the story. Have students find and make a list of the sound words. Have students sort the words into scary/not scary categories. Invite students to add new "night noises" to the list and then use these words in a class poem about the night.

Owl Moon by Jane Yolen
This story tells of a child's nighttime walk with his father and is enhanced by descriptive vocabulary. Read aloud the story as written, and then retell it with ordinary words. Invite students to discuss the differences.

Pete's Street Beat by Margaret Allen (Creative Teaching Press)
In this book silly dinosaurs describe the sights and sounds of a street fair. Invite students to discuss how the author's rhymes and sounds make the story interesting. Encourage students to brainstorm an activity and the environmental sounds that go with it. Invite students to use these environmental sounds in their writing about that activity. This book also focuses on the *ee, e-e, ea,* and ending *e* phonemes.

Rain Drop Splash by Alvin Tresselt
Read aloud this sound-filled book on a rainy day, and then invite the class to listen to and describe the rainy-day sounds they hear around them. Then invite students to brainstorm what they might hear during other kinds of weather.

Twice as Nice by Margaret Allen (Creative Teaching Press)
In this book two mice in playful competition find out their friendship is most important. Invite students to read through the book and then replace the repeated phrase (*twice as nice, twice as sweet, twice as good,* etc.) with new vocabulary from a thesaurus or class word list. This book also focuses on the *i-e* phoneme.

The Whales' Song by Dyan Sheldon
In this story Lilly's grandmother tells of waiting for whales as a child. Lilly believes the whales will come to her. The word choice captures the reader's attention. The first time you read the story, substitute common vocabulary. Then immediately reread the story as it is written. Invite students to discuss their reactions and include new vocabulary in their writing.